D1568433

The Gardens
of Mughul India

Sylvia Crowe

The Persian Background – The Mughuls in India and Kashmir

Sheila Haywood

The Indian Background – The Emperors and their Gardens

Susan Jellicoe

Research and photographs

Gordon Patterson

Land and Water: Iran, North India and Kashmir
Measured drawings

The Gardens
of Mughul India

A history
and a guide

Thames and Hudson

A tribute
to
Constance Villiers-Stuart

Contents

Map of surviving gardens

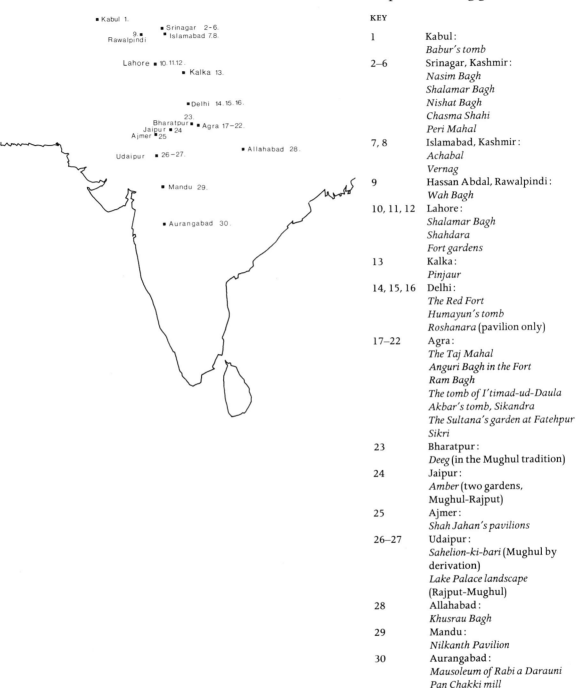

■ Kabul 1.

■ Srinagar 2–6.
9. ■
Rawalpindi ■ Islamabad 7.8.

Lahore ■ 10.11.12.
■ Kalka 13.

■ Delhi 14.15.16.
23.
Bharatpur ■ Agra 17–22.
Jaipur ■ 24
Ajmer ■ 25

■ Allahabad 28.

Udaipur ■ 26–27.

■ Mandu 29.

■ Aurangabad 30.

KEY

1	Kabul: *Babur's tomb*
2–6	Srinagar, Kashmir: *Nasim Bagh* *Shalamar Bagh* *Nishat Bagh* *Chasma Shahi* *Peri Mahal*
7, 8	Islamabad, Kashmir: *Achabal* *Vernag*
9	Hassan Abdal, Rawalpindi: *Wah Bagh*
10, 11, 12	Lahore: *Shalamar Bagh* *Shahdara* *Fort gardens*
13	Kalka: *Pinjaur*
14, 15, 16	Delhi: *The Red Fort* *Humayun's tomb* *Roshanara* (pavilion only)
17–22	Agra: *The Taj Mahal* *Anguri Bagh in the Fort* *Ram Bagh* *The tomb of I'timad-ud-Daula* *Akbar's tomb, Sikandra* *The Sultana's garden at Fatehpur Sikri*
23	Bharatpur: *Deeg* (in the Mughul tradition)
24	Jaipur: *Amber* (two gardens, Mughul-Rajput)
25	Ajmer: *Shah Jahan's pavilions*
26–27	Udaipur: *Sahelion-ki-bari* (Mughul by derivation) *Lake Palace landscape* (Rajput-Mughul)
28	Allahabad: *Khusrau Bagh*
29	Mandu: *Nilkanth Pavilion*
30	Aurangabad: *Mausoleum of Rabi a Darauni* *Pan Chakki mill*

Foreword

To Constance Villiers-Stuart, who first interested a whole generation in the Mughul gardens, we owe a debt of gratitude, since it was her inspiration which first led us to Kashmir. Her book, *Gardens of the Great Mughals*, published in 1913, is still a classic and has been our guide; her daughter, Mrs Nemon-Stuart, has kindly allowed us to use some of Mrs Villiers-Stuart's original material and to reproduce one of her water-colours.

The Archaeological Surveys in the India Office Library have provided a wealth of information upon the condition of the gardens at various times. Many had fallen into considerable disrepair by the latter part of the nineteenth century and we feel that it is not perhaps sufficiently realized today how much is owed, both to Lord Curzon and to the Archaeological Survey, for years of discerning work on the restoration of historic buildings and gardens.

Our solution to the vexed question of the spelling of names has been to adopt that of the Imperial Gazetteer for place-names and of the *Cambridge History of India* for the names of people, with two exceptions. We cannot bring ourselves to spell Taj (or indeed any other) Mahal with two 'l's; and since this is a book for the general reader we have omitted the diacritic marks over the vowels. Names which occur in direct quotations are spelt as in the original.

We should like to thank the many people who have helped us in the preparation of this book. For their advice and help in research we are greatly indebted to Professor R. A. Humphreys, and through him to the libraries of the Royal Historical Society and the School of Oriental and African Studies; to Mrs M. Archer and the India Office Library; Mr R. Skelton, Victoria and Albert Museum; Miss N. Titley, British Museum; and to Mr R. D. C. Desmond, Librarian at the Royal Botanic Gardens, Kew. We also thank Mary de Chazal, Susan Smith, Elizabeth Thomas and Peter Veitch who helped with the drawings.

To all those who helped us in Kashmir, and especially Haji Butt, our warmest thanks.

Illustrations of material in the India Office Library are reproduced by courtesy of the Secretary of State for Foreign and Commonwealth Affairs, the flower illustrations from the Roxburgh collection by permission of the Controller of H.M. Stationery Office and of the

Director, Royal Botanic Gardens, Kew. Miniatures in the British Museum are reproduced by courtesy of the Trustees.

We have drawn extensively on A. Rogers' translation of the *Memoirs of Jahangir* and to a lesser extent on Annette Beveridge's translation of the *Humayun-nama*; we are grateful to the Royal Asiatic Society for allowing us to do so. Mr John Bowen has given permission to quote his translation of Nur Jahan's epitaph from *The Golden Pomegranate* (John Baker Ltd). The three sketches by Peter Mundy are from the Rawlinson MS A.315 in the Bodleian Library, Oxford, who have kindly agreed to their being reproduced. Permission to quote from their publications has also been given by the Hakluyt Society and Cambridge University Press (*The travels of Peter Mundy, The travels of Sebastien Manrique* and *Narrative of the Embassy of Ruy Gonzales de Clavijo to the Court of Timour*); Luzac & Co. (*The Babur-nama in English*, translated by Annette Beveridge); the Asiatic Society of Calcutta (vol. 3 of H. Beveridge's translation of the *Akbar-nama*); John Murray (*Storia do Mogor*); Oxford University Press (*Early travels in India*); Panjab University Press (*Lahore past and present*).

Dramatis Personae

The Emperors, their Wives and Families, their Advisers and Chroniclers

BABUR 1508–1530	First Mughul Emperor; writer of his own Memoirs. Born 1483; conquered Delhi 1526
Maham	His wife, mother of Humayun
Zahara	His daughter, for whom he built a garden
Khvaja Kilan	His Governor in Kabul, who cared for Babur's gardens in his absence
HUMAYUN 1530–1556	Emperor, son of Babur, born 1508
Hamida Begam	His wife, mother of Akbar
Gulbadan Begam	Daughter of Babur, half-sister of Humayun, writer of the *Humayun-nama*
AKBAR 1556–1605	Emperor, son of Humayun, born 1542, said to have been called Akbar after the Ak bushes of his birthplace
Jodh Bai	His wife, a Rajput princess, mother of Jahangir, entitled Mariam-uz-Zamani after her death
Abu-'l-Fazl ibn Mubarak	Akbar's friend and chronicler, writer of the *Ain-i-Akbari* and the *Akbar-nama*; murdered at Jahangir's instigation
JAHANGIR 1605–1627	Emperor, son of Akbar, born 1569, formerly Prince Salim; writer of his own Memoirs
Jagat Gosayini	His wife, a Rajput princess, mother of Shah Jahan
Nur Jahan	His wife, widow of Sher Afgan: a Persian
Asaf Khan	Brother of Nur Jahan, father of Mumtaz Mahal; one of Jahangir's principal ministers
Ghiyas Beg	Father of Nur Jahan and Asaf Khan. Received the title of I'timad-ud-Daula
SHAH JAHAN 1628–1658	Emperor, son of Jahangir, born 1592, formerly Prince Khurram, deposed by his son Aurangzib, died 1666

Mumtaz Mahal	His wife, in whose memory he built the Taj Mahal; mother of Dara Shukoh, Shah Suja, Aurangzib and Murad : a Persian
A 'Azzu-un-nisa	His wife, who built the Shalamar Bagh, Delhi
Dara Shukoh	His son and heir, executed by Aurangzib
Jahanara Begam	His daughter, who shared his captivity
'Ali Mardan Khan	His Comptroller of Works
AURANGZIB 1658–1707	Emperor, son of Shah Jahan, born 1618
Roshanara Begam	Daughter of Shah Jahan and supporter of Aurangzib
Fadai Khan	Foster-brother of Aurangzib; laid out a garden at Pinjaur

European travellers and writers

Peter Mundy	In the service of the East India Company
William Finch	Of the East India Company
Sir Thomas Roe	Ambassador of James I at the court of Jahangir
François Bernier	A French physician
Niccolao Manucci	A gentleman of fortune, probably Venetian
Jean Baptista Tavernier	A French jeweller
Fray Sebastien Manrique	A Portuguese missionary

Chronology

The dress and extravagance of the Mughuls appear no more exotic than those of contemporary Europeans, as this miniature from Dara Shukoh's Album shows (c. 1633–4).

13

THE PERSIAN BACKGROUND

When the Mongol followers of Jenghis Khan invaded Persia in the thirteenth century, they found there a civilization 2,000 years old. Throughout her history, Persia had endured wars and invasions from Greeks, Byzantines and Turks and in A D 642 she was annexed by the Arabs to become part of their great Muslim empire. Yet, throughout this turbulence, a recognizable Persian tradition of art and living survived.

Originally the name Persia was given only to the area in the southwest of modern Iran which borders on the Persian Gulf. In the sixth century B C this area was the heart of the empire ruled by Cyrus and Darius and had as its chief cities Persepolis and Pasargadae. Later, the name Persia was applied to the whole Achaemenid empire, extending from Greece and Egypt on the west to the Indus valley and the Hindu Kush on the east. Thanks to able administration and a superb system of communications, this empire lasted for nearly two centuries until its conquest, circa 330 B C, by Alexander the Great introduced a westernized culture which long outlived Alexander's empire. The continuation of western ideas after the collapse of Alexander's empire in 250 B C was due to the fact that the new rulers were nomadic Parthians, who, with little cultural background of their own, readily adopted Hellenic civilization.

Early in the second century A D a new Persian dynasty arose. The Sassanian Ardashir I founded an empire which, though not extending as far westwards as that of the Achaemenids, again spread eastwards as far as Kabul. This empire virtually came to an end in the middle of the seventh century when it fell a prey to the Arabs, carrying all before them in the name of Islam. Between A D 642 and the Mongol invasion in 1220, Persia was ruled, nominally under the Baghdad Caliphate, by a series of minor dynasties, the last of which were the Khwarizm Shahs. But by then the whole area as far east as present-day Afghanistan had become impregnated with Persian ideas and Persian culture, accepted alike by conquerors and conquered.

Perhaps the power to assimilate invaders into her own culture which Persia possesses is due to the cosmopolitan character which has been forced upon her by geography. Lying astride the route of trade and conquest from east to west, this land cannot be by-passed by history. Not only nomadic hordes, but also the caravans trading down the great Silk Road to China, flowed through the country.

Garden carpet (Persian, 17th–18th century), showing the four rivers of life meeting in the centre, with a cartouche taking the place of the central pavilion. Cypresses and fruit trees symbolize immortality and rebirth.

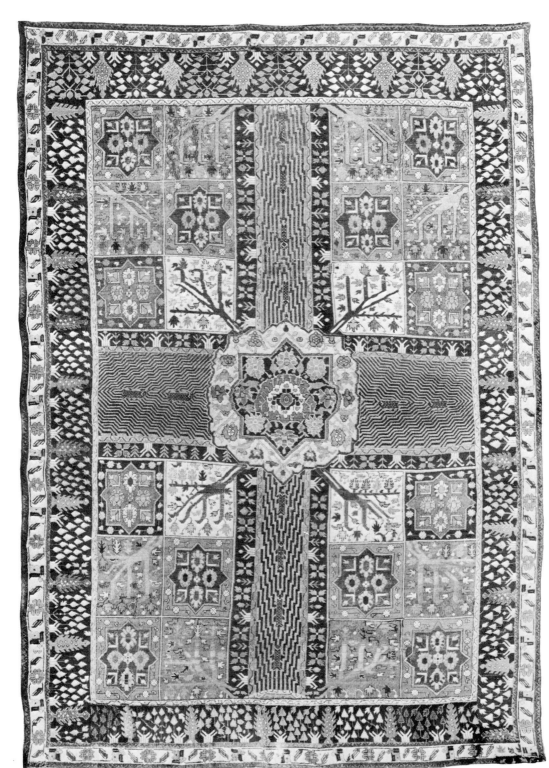

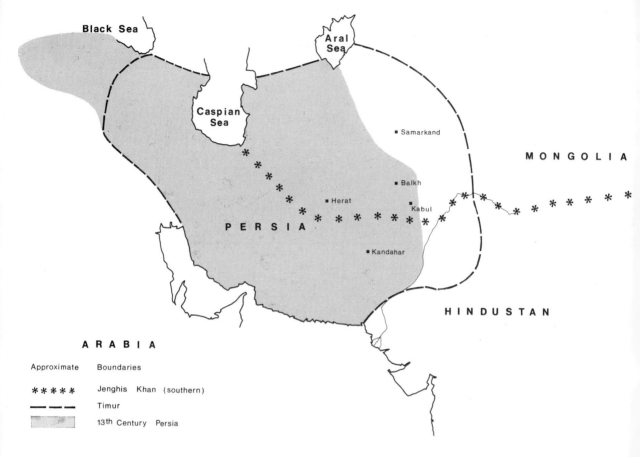

Black Sea

Aral Sea

Caspian Sea

■ Samarkand

MONGOLIA

■ Balkh

■ Herat

■ Kabul

PERSIA

■ Kandahar

HINDUSTAN

ARABIA

Approximate   Boundaries

* * * *   Jenghis   Khan   (southern)

———   Timur

13th Century   Persia

*Map showing the incursions of Jenghis Khan
and Timur Leng in the 13th and 14th
centuries. The shaded area represents the
Persian sphere of influence: Persia proper was
confined to the south-west corner.*

Consequently, conquerors did not come as strangers; contact had already been made through trade and skirmishes and it was Persia's strength that, while the influences of both east and west were absorbed, to her great enrichment, the main strand of her culture persisted. This was particularly true of her tradition of a settled life with all its possibilities for the development of the arts of living, in contrast to the nomads who drifted across her land.

An enduring part of Persian art and tradition was the paradise-park or the paradise garden, a concept which goes far back into history and which was linked from the earliest times with a deep love of trees and flowers. Xenophon, writing in 401 BC, describes how Cyrus the younger planted a garden with his own hands, carefully setting out the straight lines of trees. Earlier still, the love of trees, which was to become a passion with the Mughuls, was already felt by Xerxes, who so admired a chenar tree that he hung gold amulets upon its branches. It is recorded that Khusru II in AD 590 made a paradise of three hundred acres, and the remains of paradise gardens have been found dating back to the end of the Umayyad dynasty in AD 750. But while Persian tradition has been one of the main forces in the evolution of the paradise garden, its origins are far older than the Persian empire. It is indeed described in the Book of Genesis: 'And a river went out of Eden to water the garden; and from thence it was parted and became into four heads.' Here is the basic essence of a garden, the meeting place of spiritual and material things, wedding the practical needs of irrigation and protection with religious symbolism.

The basic design of the paradise garden is very simple. It is an idealized form of the pattern of irrigation, in which water is shown symbolically and physically as the source of life. In its primitive form, water-channels, representing the four rivers of life, cross in the centre of the garden, dividing the rectangular area into four quarters. These water-courses are raised above the level of the surrounding ground, as they must be to serve the purpose of irrigation; on each side of the channels and irrigated by their water, are straight lines of trees, while the quarters may also be filled with trees and flowers. Sometimes the trees extend at each side of the garden to form a park or woodland. The whole is surrounded by a wall to keep out the surrounding desert with its dust-laden winds and to give privacy and protection. From the basic design there developed many variations and embellishments. For instance a pavilion was often set at the intersection of the main channels, where the coolness from the water could best be enjoyed.

The cross, formed by the intersection of the water-channels, has been the symbol of the meeting of humanity and God in many religions, and water itself is a symbol as well as a necessity of life. A more complex symbol, not found in the earlier paradise gardens but much used by the Mughuls, is the octagon; evolved from the squaring of the circle, it symbolizes the reconciliation of the material side

The Friday Mosque, Isfahan. The brimming waters of the Mughul gardens are a feature of ablution tanks throughout the Muslim world.

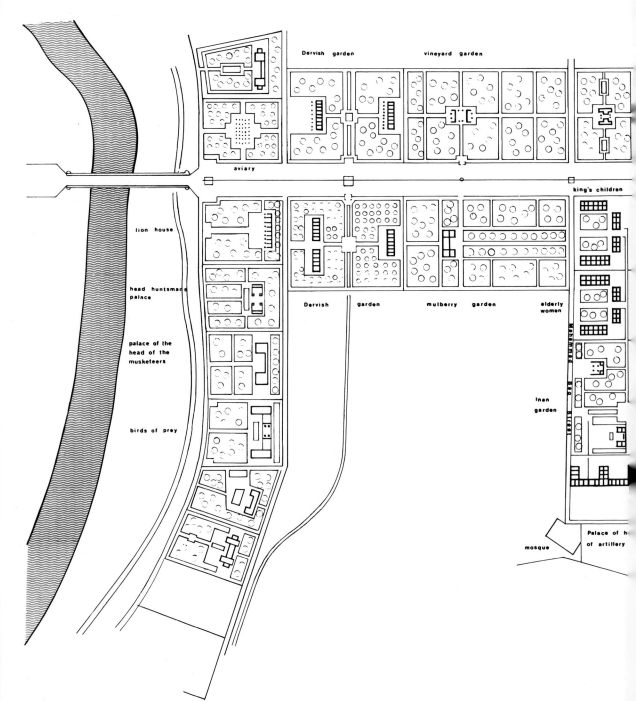

Dervish garden

vineyard garden

aviary

lion house

head huntsmans palace

palace of the head of the musketeers

birds of prey

king's children

Dervish   garden

mulberry   garden

elderly women

Inan garden

mosque

Palace of h of artillery

Plan of Isfahan as laid out by the Safavid Shah
Abbas, who moved his capital there in 1598.
The spine of the design is the long, wide
avenue called Chahar Bagh (Four Gardens),
once the royal pleasure gardens.

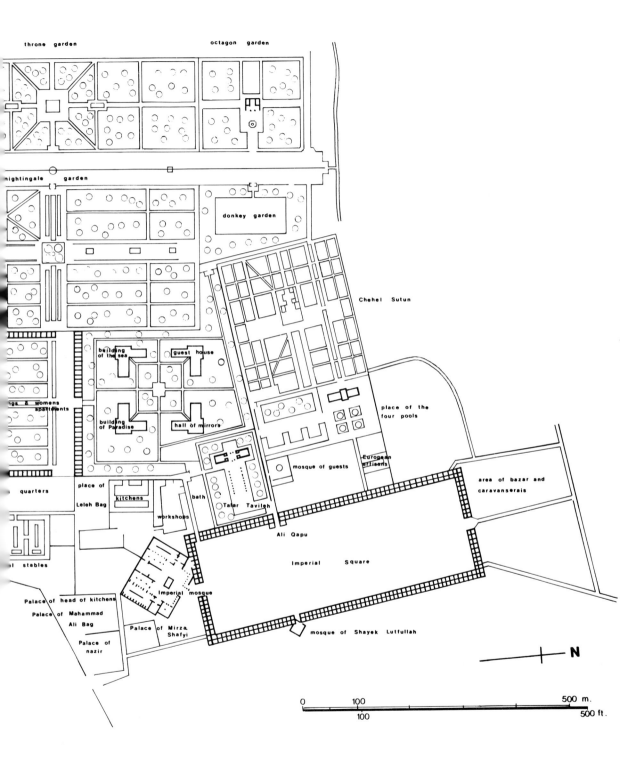

throne garden

octagon garden

nightingale garden

donkey garden

Chehel Sutun

building of the sea

guest house

place of the four pools

building of Paradise

hall of mirrors

gs & womens apartments

European artisans

mosque of guests

area of bazar and caravanserais

quarters

place of Leleh Bag

kitchens

bath

Talar Tavileh

workshops

Ali Qapu

al stables

Imperial   Square

Palace of head of kitchens

Palace of Mahammad Ali Bag

Imperial mosque

Palace of Mirza Shafyi

Palace of nazir

mosque of Shayek Lutfullah

N

0   100   500 m.

100   500 ft.

19

Dovecotes at the corners of walled gardens on the Iranian plateau are ancestors of the Mughul gazebos. Made of mud brick, they form an integral part of the wall of the cultivated enclosure which lies beyond.

of man, represented by the square, with the circle of eternity. In the later Persian garden, and still more in those of the Mughuls, other forms of Muslim symbolism played their part. Gardens divided into eight parts represented the eight divisions of the Qoran, while the frequent references by the Mughul garden-makers to constructing their water-tanks ten cubits by ten cubits originates in the religious significance of this measurement, which was that prescribed for ablution tanks, in whose brimming waters the faithful must wash before making their devotions. In the traditional planting of alternate cypress and fruit trees along the water-ways immortality was symbolized by the evergreen cypress and the renewal of life by the spring flowering trees.

A characteristic of all Muslim gardens is the way in which their geometric symmetry is interlaced and overlaid with the freedom of plant growth. Spring flowers grow informally from the exact turf plot, roses spray over the water-tanks, trees branch in their natural forms. The intellectual concept of geometric order is wedded to the freedom of organic growth.

The prototype of the paradise garden is flat, but in Persia water-falls were introduced where the gardens stood on the sides of the hills rising from the plain, as they did at Shiraz. Another common Persian feature was the existence of dove-cotes at the corners of the encircling walls, examples of which can still be seen in the country-side near Isfahan. These were for the utilitarian purpose of providing protein, but they have an affinity both with the later Mughul pavilions at the corners of their walls and with the gazebos which appeared in the Tudor and Jacobean gardens of England of about the same date as many of the gardens of Shiraz and Isfahan.

Though the paradise garden is not a uniquely Persian idea it developed there more fruitfully than anywhere else, and became a tradition which persisted through all invasions and political upheavals, strong enough to inspire offshoots in far-distant lands where the pattern inflected to new conditions without losing its essential characteristics. It is probable that the crusaders brought back the idea of the paradise garden to France and England, in whose medieval gardens a well or tank was all that remained of the water of life, placed at the centre crossing of the paths which divided the paradise garden into its four quarters. A more virile offshoot can be seen in the Moorish gardens of southern Spain, which came to perfection at Granada under Arab rule. But the greatest offshoot of all, and the one most closely influenced by Persia herself, was the garden tradition of the Great Mughuls.

The ebb and flow of nomads across Persia was relevant in many ways to the development of the Mughul arts in India in the sixteenth and seventeenth centuries, for the Central Asian invaders of India passed first through Persia, and carried with them into India some echoes of Iranian culture. Graeco-Iranian influences persisted in Afghanistan and India long after the fall of Alexander, and can be seen especially in coins and sculpture. Even Roman details, such as pilasters, may be found on the early Hindu temples of Kashmir. India in turn transmitted westwards influences from the Far East. This interchange of Indo-Iranian culture reached its zenith as early as the Gupta period in the third century A D. There was therefore already a strong Iranian element in Rajput art before the coming of the Mughuls. The direct Mughul debt is however to Islamic Iran, to the Muslim ideals of order, and to their poets, who had for centuries celebrated nature and the garden.

The Mughuls had a long history of contact with Persia, dating back to the invasions of their Mongol ancestors in A D 1220, culminating in the conquests of Timur Leng (Tamerlane or Tamberlane) and the founding of the Timurid Empire in the fourteenth century. This empire extended from the Mediterranean to India. When Timur captured Samarkand he carried to the city artists from Baghdad and Shiraz, who brought with them the finest art traditions of Persia. Descriptions of the gardens he made there were recorded by Ruy Gonzales de Clavijo, who was sent as ambassador to Timur's court in 1403–6:

'The ambassadors went to see a chamber which the lord (Timur Beg) had set apart for feasting and for the company of his women. In front of it there was a great garden, in which were many shady trees and all kinds of fruit trees, with channels of water flowing amongst them. The garden was so large, that great numbers of people might enjoy themselves there in the summer with great delight, near the fountains and under the shade of the trees.'

Clavijo also mentions gardens set with tents, some of red cloth, others of embroidered silk.

Five generations later Timur's descendant, Babur, first of the Mughul emperors, described in his journal the gardens of Samarkand, recording that Timur brought stone-cutters from Hindustan to work on his Friday mosque. He also planted a great avenue of white poplars.

The Timurid Empire broke up in 1500 but its influence remained and Babur grew up in an atmosphere imbued with Persian tradition and a love of art and gardens. In his youth he visited Samarkand, whose ruler, an uncle of Babur's, had laid out gardens with such seductive titles as 'The Perfect Garden' and 'The Heart-Delighting'. These made a deep and lasting impression. He visited Herat in Khorasan as well, then a great cultural centre, where another royal kinsman, Sultan Husain Baiqara, had also laid out many gardens. Husain was a great patron of the arts and Persian poets and artists flocked to his court. He ruled from 1487 to 1506 and was thus the contemporary of Lorenzo de' Medici and Leonardo da Vinci. From these early contacts and traditions Babur carried the ideals of Persian art and way of life into the territories of northern India, where after his conquest in 1526 he founded the Mughul dynasty.

The Mughul empire formed one chapter in India's long history of changing dynasties. To appreciate the achievements of the Mughuls it is necessary to have some understanding of the Indian background, and the influence which it had upon them and their art.

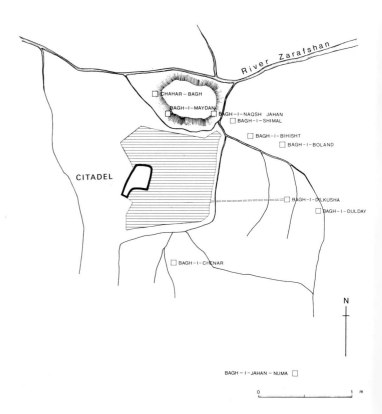

Map of gardens round Samarkand in the 15th century.

THE INDIAN BACKGROUND

India has known many civilizations, and has seen many rulers, native and alien, come and go. Nearly all have been in varying degrees despotic, whether benevolent or otherwise. Since the eighth century north-west India had been increasingly dominated by the Rajput clans. Warlike and aristocratic, their unity was less one of race than of caste and intermarriage. Yet the Rajputs were a part only of countless Hindu states and kingdoms, pursuing their courses in comparative isolation and often almost unaware of events in other parts of India. Amongst them, in the twelfth century, Muslim power made its appearance in the person of Muhammad of Ghur (originally an obscure Afghan principality). His successors established the Sultanate of Delhi, which lasted from 1206 to 1526, although declining rapidly in power after 1340.

In the background of Central Asia there remained the ominous figures of the Mongols. Under their leader Jenghis Khan (1162–1227), they had swept relentlessly from China to the Black Sea, leaving behind such a fearful reputation as has seldom been equalled. India was spared the worst, since on reaching the Indus Jenghis Khan turned his attention elsewhere, but the country was harried by constant Mongol raids; in 1241 Lahore was sacked. Later, in the fourteenth century, Timur Leng, a Barlas Turk, created in the Timurid Empire a new image of terror and splendour. In 1398 he in turn sacked Delhi, leaving it in ruin and confusion, and carrying away not only its treasures but virtually all its skilled workmen to his own capital at Samarkand. The Sultanate subsequently crumbled, to be destroyed finally by the Mughul invasions.

During its existence, two profoundly differing cultures had already been brought into contact with one another.

Earlier Hindu art was centred upon the temple and the multiplicity of deities involved. It was based on a concept of organic growth, on the rhythms of nature and of humanity, always complex and individual. Sculpture was the natural expression of such beliefs, and the temples themselves related perhaps more nearly to sculpture than to any architectural approach to building. Ornament consisted largely of statues, carvings and bas-reliefs, which portrayed subjects both religious and temporal. Nature and the human figure appeared in increasingly lifelike groupings of great beauty and often of surprising eroticism. Flowers and plants, especially the lotus, were a part of worship, and were shown in intricate detail in the carvings.

The temple of Kandariya Mahadeo, Khajuraho, dedicated c. AD 1000. The original group of 85 temples to which this belongs was the culminating achievement of Indo-Aryan genius in architecture.

23

Much less is known of secular buildings or gardens, probably due to the devastating effects of flooding upon a largely mud-brick construction, though there are traces of a contrasting geometry in the polygonal work of hill forts. Within the temples immense riches in the form of gold and jewels accumulated, a temptation to future invaders.

The Muslims by contrast brought with them a culture rooted in the desert and the oasis. It was compounded from abstract principles of order, mathematics and law, and above all from a profound belief in the unity of God. Their designs were geometric, relying on calculated division and subdivision, and upon enclosure from a hostile environment. In decoration, flowers and calligraphy were woven into abstract patterns, while colours were clear and brilliant. Human and animal figures were unacceptable on religious buildings and rare upon others.

The meeting of these two fundamentally different conceptions of life and art resulted in a fusion of Indo-Islamic themes from which the Mughuls in turn enriched their own designs. The Sultans of Delhi had based their mosques and madrassehs (theological colleges) on Muslim ideas. But as a ruling minority they were dependent on Hindu craftsmen, who exerted their own influences and contributed an organic quality far removed from the mathematical exactitudes of their rulers. The temptations offered by the treasures in the Hindu temples meanwhile led to much destruction, and their materials were often carried off for use in Muslim buildings. The Qutb mosque at Delhi, for instance, is said to have incorporated materials ransacked from twenty-seven Hindu temples. Among the Sultans, Firuz Shah (1351–88) was notable both for his enlightened attitude towards building and for his religious toleration. He built forts, towns and mosques, as well as embankments, canals and gardens. Unusual too, in his day, was the considerable effort he devoted to the restoration of earlier buildings, for the general tendency in that period was to be wholly destructive of the past. Some of his canals survived to be put to new uses by the Mughuls, but of his gardens little but the memory remains.

Such was the background to the Mughul invasions, which, after initial skirmishes, began in earnest in 1525. The first three reigns saw the Mughul territories expand, almost vanish, and then expand again to cover more than half India. From its beginnings at Agra, Babur's empire at his death had reached from Badakshan to Benares and Patna. His son Humayun was no match for his Afghan rival, Sher Khan Sur, and fled into Persia, returning to recapture Delhi and Agra only after Sher Khan's death. The Afghan was both a remarkable leader of men and a capable administrator. Throughout the large regions which he subdued, he laid the foundations of sound government from which Akbar, Humayun's son and successor, was later to benefit, and left behind him not only many fine buildings, but extensive roads and tree-planting, together with the provision of wells and *sarais* (rest-houses) for travellers.

From the nucleus at Delhi and Agra which remained at Humayun's death, the empire expanded once again under Akbar's generalship

Opposite: The founders of the Mughul Empire, Babur, Timur Leng and Humayun (seated). The Mongols may be defined as the savage followers of Jenghis Khan, the 'narrow-eyed people'. The Mughuls, more settled and civilized, were partly of Turkish origin and had become Muslims. Mongols and Mughuls had however freely intermarried, and Mongol characteristics, especially the 'narrow eyes', often appear in earlier Mughul portraits.

The Qutb Minar, standing in the enclosure of the Quwat-ul-islam mosque in old Delhi. The whole complex was begun in 1196 by Qutb-ud-din Aibak, one of Muhammad of Ghur's generals, who succeeded Muhammad as Sultan of Delhi. The great minaret has an organic quality all its own.

The old palace at Amber, Jaipur. A garden in the zenana quarters. Rajput and Mughul influences reacted the one upon the other.

to reach from Kabul and Kashmir to the Deccan and the Bay of Bengal. His dominions now included widely differing regions, and subjects of many origins and religions. Rajput influences, centred on Delhi and Agra, were the first to affect design. Their craftsmen were employed on the Mughul buildings, and perhaps more significantly, Akbar's marriage with a Rajput princess carried the Rajput blood into the dynasty itself.

Rajput art already showed considerable Iranian elements: comparatively plain surfaces contrasted with incised decorations, plaited or spiral ornament, and stylized figures and animals. Local building materials were also an important factor, since stone was limited to a comparatively few areas. The earlier Mughul garden-palaces derived their unique flavour perhaps most from colour. The subtle low-toned reds and yellows of the Hindus, the use of red sandstone and insets of black-and-white marble or blue schist made a considerable departure from the clear-cut Persian colours. Hindu motives appeared in such details as lintels, columns, eaves, fretted balconies or lotus rondels, while carving was rich with flowers and animals, flower scrolls being combined with Muslim inscriptions. Akbar's work at the Agra Fort was a *tour-de-force* of red sandstone, vigorously carved, while at Fatehpur Sikri much of the actual planning is tortuous and irregular, a far cry from Muslim concepts of order.

In gardens, the Rajput heritage is perhaps most clearly seen at Amber, near Jaipur, the home of Akbar's Rajput wife, mother of Jahangir who became the next emperor. These, with their romantic lake and hillside settings, their strange combination of the exact and the picturesque, perfectly express the union of widely separated ideals. The stone parterres in the two more important Amber gardens are based upon the star, which was held in special esteem by the Seljuk Turks, for whom it stood for life itself, and for man's intellectual powers. It may be significant that immigrants of Turkish origin had at one time taken refuge in Rajputana.

Later the white marble architecture of Gujarat, one of Akbar's most important conquests, came to have an increasing impact, until the central buildings in any important garden were almost always of white marble. Kashmir too exerted its own special influences in the knowledge and use of flower decoration, and at least one Kashmiri name is recorded among the craftsmen of the Taj Mahal.

So, from different strands of different cultures: Indo-Islamic, Rajput, Gujarati, Kashmiri, the great Mughul gardens evolved, with always the Persian connection linking the whole together.

Amber. A lake garden seen from one of the zenana windows.

LAND AND WATER:
Iran, North India, Kashmir

While Persia is divided into several geophysical, climatic and vegetational regions, the dominant land form of central Iran is an elevated plateau, in the shape of a basin, surrounded by ranges of higher mountains. These are largely of alpine origin, rising sharply and steeply from the plain. Only in the north-east does the land change markedly in character. Here, from the high Elburz mountains down to the shores of the Caspian, the climate is mediterranean, with all that this implies – lush vegetation, high rainfall, and a more temperate climate. Yet it is the more arid central areas which have most influenced the patterns both of irrigation and of garden design.

The reasons can perhaps best be appreciated from the air by the modern traveller. To the nomads who for centuries threaded its deserts it may well have presented widely differing aspects and colours, but seen from above, there is a monochromatic theme which is seldom relieved. The colour, red-brown, changes in tone only where open plateau gives way to surrounding foot-hills or steeper mountains, where shadows help to enliven an otherwise flat landscape. Even where land changes to water, the reds are never contrasted with greys or blues, but merge into yellower shades, for the lagoons are formed from slow-moving brackish rivers.

Much of Iran is empty, with scarcely a sign of vegetation, though within this apparent and largely illusionary emptiness we know there to be numerous centres of lively prosperity, and there is a whole range of agricultural enterprise forming an important part of the nation's economy. The answer to how this can flourish is to be found in the water supply. Until relatively recent times a supply of natural water lay at the heart of civilization in this and many other parts of Asia. For many peoples it still does. Not only has an adequate water supply provided a means of progression from nomadic wandering to highly sophisticated social units such as are seen in the cities of Tehran or Shiraz, but this quest for water has produced within the Persian mind a deep-lying philosophy and respect for its life-giving quality which pervades and influences many of their far-reaching achievements.

Before the oil industry arrived, cities, towns and villages developed on the fertile oases of cultivated and watered lands, which were dependent upon the various systems of irrigation devised by the Persians. From these, agricultural and garden patterns have evolved, in turn giving rise to techniques and designs which have spread far beyond the confines of Central Asia.

An artificial canal, constructed from one of the tributaries of the Zaindeh river. Corn, poplar and willow grow freely on the banks.

A narrow stone canal or juke bringing water to a village from a nearby river. The sarai in the background provides shelter for both travellers and their animals.

A cemetery and orchard in the Zaindeh river oasis south of Isfahan. The water channel which feeds the garden enclosure can be seen crossing the ploughland below wall.

Water has provided the *raison d'être* for a whole series of garden layouts for which the traditional Persian methods of irrigation have been used. There are the well gardens, the canal gardens, the tank gardens, as well as all those gardens relying for their effect upon changes of levels and subdivisions of land invariably dictated by a water landscape. These elements have been used not so much because they provide decorative features but rather that without them and the water (which is systematically used and re-used) the gardens themselves could not and would not exist. They would succumb to the intensity of the searing sun. The water, if not quickly replenished by some means or other, would be completely dissipated and lost as the result of the evaporation or seepage. An enquiry into the source of such supplies of water, both for agricultural purposes and for garden-making, is therefore an important step towards an understanding of the basic patterns taken on by so many of these gardens.

In the central desert area the climate is continental and the rainfall seldom exceeds five inches in the year, most of which falls within a short space of time. It is not unusual for Isfahan, roughly at the centre of the plateau, to have four of its five inches of rain all within one day. Since the mountains are young and steep-sided, the run-off, other than for melting snows, is very rapid. Few rivers exist permanently: with exceptionally high evaporation and seepage through the shaly, porous ground, little water remains at the surface for long. The concentrated and sporadic downpours are such that relatively little rain is confined within the river courses and there is a great tendency for it to flood out over the land, often devastating everything that gets in the way. For these reasons as much as for the conservation of water itself, much time and ingenuity have been lavished on building systems of water canalization, both for irrigation and to keep the water within bounds.

One of Iran's major rivers which survives throughout the year is the Zaindeh ('Life-giving') River, flowing through Isfahan. Life it indeed gives to the whole of the fertile oasis surrounding it. This extends for some forty miles, ten to fifteen miles across at its widest. The waters of the Zaindeh derive from the high Zagros mountains in the west which, like the Elburz mountains to the north, are snow-covered all the year round. The waters of this river persist through many hundreds of miles before finally losing themselves in the Gavkaneh salts flats to the east.

Above its banks, particularly in the neighbourhood of Isfahan, an entirely agricultural landscape has been developed, which is in sharp and marked contrast to the desert that lies beyond it. The change from one to the other is dramatic and extremely clear cut. Along the upper stretches of the river, where it flows strongest, the water is conducted by small aqueducts or jukes, away from the main flow, to take it within urban and village communities. It is these water-courses or jukes that form such a familiar feature of many Persian towns, even of Tehran itself.

Early settlers lived happily where the environment was most favourable, for example upon the river bank, but later the less desirable and more difficult areas had to be pressed into use once the more fertile tracts of land became more populated. Isfahan owes its success only in part to the river and its subsidiary irrigation canals which are derived from it. It is also dependent upon two other forms of water device: first, the well-hole, and, second, a particular type of well known as a *qanat*.

The Persian well, where water is raised by a series of scoops fixed to a moving belt stretched between two wheels, is familiar. The mechanism was often operated by harnessed animals – mules, asses and oxen – driving a rotary yoke or, less frequently, by treadmill. The *qanat* or underground tunnel-well is, however, less well known. This particular method of conducting water from a source-well rather than raising it is essentially Persian in origin and has been used for over 2,000 years. It is supposed that the ancient city of Persepolis (500 BC) was supplied with water by this means. Essentially it is an underground water-way, tunnelled and channelled. Water is conducted by gravity fall, in some cases over very considerable distances, from water-bearing strata (usually at the foot of steep hills) to a position where it is required. The great centre of Tehran, with all its outward signs of modern civilization and westernization, is still supplied with water largely from *qanats* which have their source at the base of the Elburz mountains. In Persia as a whole there are many thousands of major *qanat* runs covering thousands of miles in length, many of which are still in active use.

To the traveller coming to Persia for the first time, the *qanat* excavations are a source of wonderment. From the air it is as if some monstrous footprints have marked the landscape. Suddenly, and without apparent reason, they appear and then, equally without reason, vanish. Yet it is these *qanats* which give rise to the quite sudden, and to some quite mysterious, appearance of green in the desert.

An aerial view of qanat *borings near Isfahan, looking like white dots with black centres. One line crosses the top left corner, another crosses the bottom right corner. To the left of the road that runs from bottom to top of the picture, a third line runs up to feed the village in the bottom left foreground.*

31

The construction of a *qanat* makes a fascinating study. When a particular source of water is located, usually by specialist diviners, say at the foot of a mountain, a vertical master shaft is dug or drilled to the level of the water, which may vary considerably but does not usually exceed about 150 feet. The depth of the level of the water below ground is then gauged and the position of the outfall on a horizontal line is estimated by means of a series of horizontal alignments and drops along the surface. A line is then drawn between the master shaft and the point of outfall, and thence to the point where the water is to be used. This establishes the course of the *qanat*.

Following this line, a series of further vertical shafts is drilled, each at a distance of twenty to thirty yards apart along this line, to such a depth as to be in horizontal alignment with the level of water at the base of the master shaft. Finally, from the bottom of each shaft a tunnel is excavated to connect each length to the next, so as to extend from the outfall back to the source of water. Ultimately, a breakthrough is made on the last section, so that the water flows along the whole of the tunnel, discharging at the outfall. Here it is usually conducted into a channel, from which it is put to various uses. Normally, the horizontal tunnel is bored through the formation strata without support, but if the ground is exceptionally shaly or liable to subsidence it may be necessary to line the excavation with brick, wood or tile. The tunnel is usually four to five feet in diameter.

Many *qanats* terminate in a tank or cistern from which water supplies for further uses may then be drawn. But more commonly the water is conducted from enclosure to enclosure by straightforward gravity feed. Highly reticulated systems of waterways are built up until every drop is drained and used up. With the introduction of new drilling techniques some *qanats* have become obsolete, but many communities still rely entirely on water supplied in this way.

From these beginnings many rectilinear agronomic patterns are derived and these patterns in turn give rise to the strongly rectilinear forms common to so many traditional Persian garden enclosures. It was the cistern or storage tank which first gave the idea for the Persian garden-tank, the crossing piece of the *char-bagh* (literally, four-gardens). In some cases it is found below ground level. Flights of steps lead to a subterranean room with an evenness of temperature which is a boon in so hot and arid a climate. Here too are seen the origins of the *birchet* or *ambar* – the resting-house, so typical a feature of the classic water garden, either astride or alongside the more formal garden canal.

Thus the gardens took on their essential form, fashioned from the factors and limitations of land and climate, and it is interesting to see how that form became modified when transported to the alien landscape of India and Kashmir by the Mughul invaders.

It was to north India that the Mughuls first took their genius for the management of water. They found a vast level land, rich and fertile, stretching northwards in apparent infinity until it stopped abruptly against the great wall of the Himalayas. The climate is dominated by the monsoon, bringing the torrential rains of summer, which are contrasted with dry hot winds for much of the remaining year.

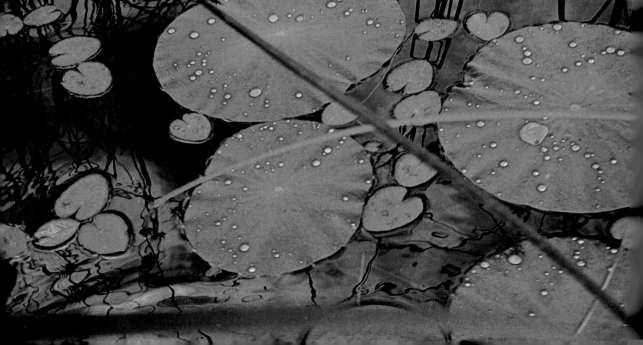

Agriculture depends largely on the monsoon: the success or failure of the rains can still mean life or death for thousands. Immense rivers, such as the Indus and the Jumna, combine with extremes of rainfall to make flooding a recurrent hazard and in addition the rivers themselves have from time to time changed their actual courses, with devastating results. At other times, heat, dust and the hot winds of which the emperor Babur was to complain so feelingly, can become intolerable. To the south lies the great plateau of the Deccan, the scene of Aurangzib's relentless military campaigns.

Irrigation, of course, was far from unknown in India when the Mughuls arrived in 1526. Previous rulers had constructed not only canals but artificial lakes, while the tradition of planting shade trees and of linking these to wells, to assist in both coolness and the conservation of water, was an ancient one. Various methods of raising water from wells and rivers were in use: the wheel, operated by either a treadmill or by yoked animals, and the lever arrangement known as a *shadoof*.

In his memoirs, Babur described at length how he extended and developed the water supply wherever he went in India and he compares critically the various versions of the water-wheel which he found in different parts of the country. In particular, he expressed his disgust at the way in which some wheels were inevitably fouled by the droppings of the animals which operated them. Later, Akbar's great city of Fatehpur Sikri was supplied with water by means of an artificial lake and a system of Persian wheels, while at his tomb at Sikandra, bullocks may be seen working a water-wheel to the present day.

The early Mughul gardens in India followed closely on their Persian origins, the level landscape dictating an almost two-dimensional form. Meanwhile, as supplies of water improved, the patterns of water-courses became increasingly intricate.

Bullocks working the water-wheel at Akbar's tomb at Sikandra, near Agra, in 1964. An ox-hide bucket is lifted by a simple pulley and drawn by yoked oxen to discharge well-water into the canal system of the garden. An inclined ramp has been constructed on one side of the well-head, so that in hauling the full buckets the oxen are pulling downhill. The bucket is the complete hide of an ox gathered at the four corners with lanyards, the water resting in the sag of the leather as it is drawn upwards from the well. The prospect is a dismal one for the ox.

COLOUR PLATES
Fountains at Achabal, Kashmir.

Lotus after rain on Lake Dal, Kashmir.

35

The carefully tended humanized landscape of the Kashmir Valley is held within the strong bastion of the Pir Panjal range. One of the routes used by the Mughul Emperors on their way up from India to Kashmir penetrated this barrier, crossing an 11,400-foot pass.

In Kashmir, conditions were almost entirely dissimilar. It is divided from the west by the high outlying ranges of the Himalayas. To north and south are the strong demarcation lines of watersheds. Only to the north-east is there a break in the mountain ranges, which leads into Tibet. In some ways there are resemblances here to the basin-like form of the central Iranian plateau, though in practically every other respect the country is very different. The greater part of Kashmir is protected from the severity of the monsoon by the Pir Panjal range: thus its climate is ideal in early summer and autumn, whilst in winter the weather is alpine and in August oppressive.

The Vale of Kashmir, tiny where Iran and India are immense, is one of nature's most fortunate creations. Some ninety miles long and twenty to twenty-five miles wide, it is watered by the River Jhelum which flows approximately south-east to north-west throughout its length before breaking through the deep gorge in the Pir Panjal range to the west.

One of the interesting aspects of the river within its richly furnished landscape and basin is the way in which the Wular lake, about twenty-five miles to the west of the capital, Srinagar, forms a grand regulating-tank. When the river is in full spate the lake can be as much as fifty to sixty square miles in area. At other times it is much smaller: nature itself pointing the method so rigorously pursued by the Persians.

Unlike in Persia, the vegetation here is prolific and even at 12,000 feet the land supports rhododendron and juniper. On the lower slopes are spruce, pines and cedars, while in the valley itself plane, poplar and willow provide the principal shade trees, and the terrain has encouraged a deep and fertile soil, built up through centuries on the valley floor. Rice is the staple crop but an immense range of other food is grown. Water is abundant, for in addition to the two great lakes, the Wular and the Dal, and the River Jhelum, there are several springs of great force and innumerable smaller streams.

Much of Lake Dal must once have been undifferentiated marsh, but, long before the Mughuls came, works of reclamation had been carried out on the wet-lands. Lagoons and canals have been scooped out and the mud used to build up bunds, or embankments, on which are grown willows for fodder, poplars for timber and crops of vegetables. One of these canals and a bund built by an earlier Muslim king, Zain-ul-Abidin, leads to Shalamar, where once a much earlier garden stood. The claiming of dry land from the wet background of the lake is like a mirror reflection of the creation of irrigation channels in the Iranian desert. Another form of land reclamation which has continued through the centuries is the formation of floating islands. These are made by cutting the vegetation in the lake and binding it together to form long, narrow rafts. Mud and more weeds are used to bind and build up the thickness and the island is moored by stakes of willow driven through it, which allow it to rise and fall with the changes of water level. It can, if required, be towed to another part of the lake. The islands are used for market-gardening and for vegetable crops. This thrifty use of land is made necessary by the narrowness of the level land between the water and the hills.

A Kashmiri painting showing traditions of horticulture. In the upper picture a boatman is picking lotus from a shikara, while in the top right-hand corner is a floating island, with melons or cucumbers planted on mounds. Below, a gardener with his tools and crops: apples, rice, lotus, melons, etc.

A green waterway leading from Srinagar to Lake Dal. The artificial bunds in the centre of the picture are planted with willow for fodder and poplars for timber. The channel is kept open and the bund repaired by scooping mud from the canal bottom. A long shovel, similar to the one in the picture above, is used by a man standing waist deep in the water.

In Kashmir the problem in designing a garden was less the supply of water than the challenge to exploit its abundance to the full. Spectacular natural waterfalls provided the prototypes for the Mughul cascades, while existing springs, such as those at Achabal and Vernag, already places of worship, became the focal points round which whole new gardens were developed. Mughuls and Kashmiris shared a reverence for water: its quality, taste and coldness were keenly appreciated and discussed.

The terrain, too, offered new opportunities. No longer did water need to be laboriously raised with wheels from the ground. Instead, the steep mountain sides provided scope for dramatic water landscapes. Powerful springs and streams, emerging from the hills, fell with increased force over chutes and waterfalls, or were disciplined into wide pools filled with fountains. Terrace succeeded terrace, as for instance at Nishat Bagh on Lake Dal, where there were no less than twelve, the lowest one discharging its waterfall triumphantly into the lake. Yet no opportunity, however small, was lost. A tiny artificial island, the Char Chenar in Lake Dal, lay only just above the water level, but at one time it contained a garden and the necessary wheel to raise the lake water sufficiently to maintain it.

The Kashmir gardens are perhaps all the more remarkable in that these tremendous works were undertaken for summer enjoyment only. This prodigality, coupled with the hazards of the mountain crossings, is a measure of Jahangir's love for the country: he lingered to the last possible moment, when snow was beginning to fall in the passes, before he could tear himself away.

Boats moored among the floating islands on Lake Dal.

Opposite: A 19th-century Kashmiri painting showing cycle of the rice crop. The labourers are working up to their knees in water.

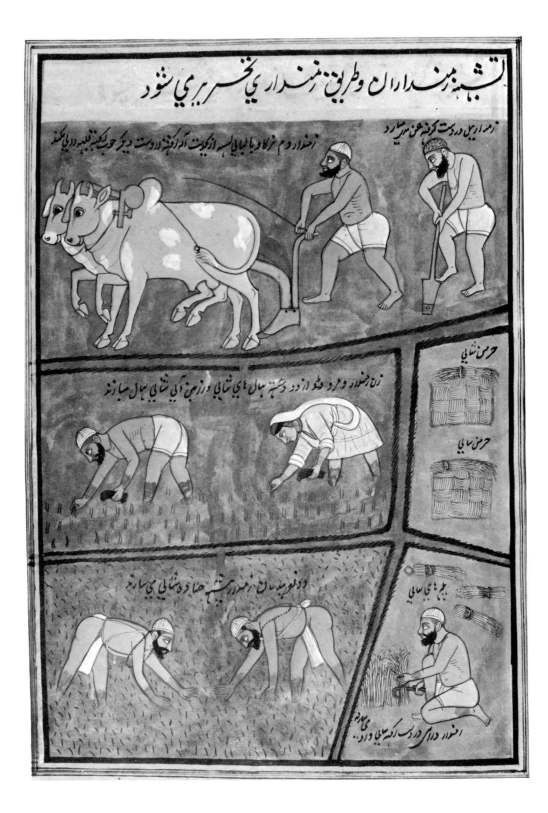

THE MUGHULS IN INDIA AND KASHMIR

The Mughul Empire in northern India lasted as an effective power from 1526 to the 1750s, although the dynasty lingered on until the defeat of Bahadur Shah II in 1857. Its greatest epoch was spread over the reigns of the six emperors from Babur to Aurangzib. During this time the successive emperors, their wives and their noblemen created innumerable gardens in northern India, Afghanistan and Kashmir. Throughout the period there was almost constant war and revolt. Yet with each succeeding emperor – at least up to the accession of Aurangzib – the making of gardens was a ruling passion.

Babur, whose life was a long history of struggle, defeats, exiles and finally hard-won victory, could still pause on his march and order plantains from the Punjab to be planted in one of his gardens in distant Kabul. Akbar, his grandson, the greatest of them all, a wise and tolerant statesman and a brilliant general, could spare time to set out plantations with his own hand.

Akbar's son, Jahangir, was even more devoted to his gardens and intensely interested in botany, observing the flowers he saw upon his marches with meticulous care. Of his visit to Kashmir in 1620 he wrote: 'Sweet smelling plants of narcissus, violet, and strange flowers that grow in this country, came to view. Among these flowers I saw one extraordinary one. It had five or six orange flowers blooming with their heads downward. From the middle of the flowers there came out some green leaves, as in the case of the pineapple.' A delightful description of a Crown Imperial.

Shah Jahan, last of the great garden builders, bequeathed the Taj Mahal to posterity. It is fitting that this culminating glory of the Mughul tradition should have been inspired by Jahan's love for his empress, Mumtaz Mahal. For the ladies of this dynasty were quite as remarkable as the men and probably more cultivated. They wielded great power, apparently enhanced rather than diminished by their Muslim seclusion.

With the Persian tradition of gardens and irrigation firmly embedded in his mind, Babur's first thought on reaching India in 1526 was to bring the blessings of water to the hot and dusty land of Hind.

'Three things oppressed us in Hindustan – its heat, its violent winds, its dust.'

Memoirs of Babur

Prince Sultan Parviz with his friends, painted by Govardhan. Carpets have been spread in front of a fountain, in a formal Mughul garden, such as still exists in the grounds of Humayun's tomb. The discussion is obviously literary.

He also brought to it the love of order and symmetry that was equally a part of the paradise garden tradition. His memoirs describe the making of a garden at Istalif in Afghanistan:

'A one-mill stream, having trees on both banks, flows constantly through the middle of the garden; formerly its course was zig-zag and irregular; I had it made straight and orderly; so the place became very beautiful.'

In both Iran and Kashmir, it is noticeable today that the agricultural irrigation channels curve with the contours of the land, but within the gardens they run straight.

In tracing the Mughul influence in India, one should neither belittle their achievements nor underrate what had been done before they came. Firuz Shah, who reigned in Firuzabad (the forerunner of Delhi) from 1351 to 1388, is credited with having built a hundred gardens. A love of flowers was as deep-rooted in India as in Persia; indeed they were necessary to the observance of both the Hindu and Buddhist religions. A far earlier tradition of temple gardens, flowery and informal, had travelled with Buddhism from India to the Far East there to fertilize the Chinese and from thence the Japanese garden, antithesis of the formal paradise garden.

The transference of ideas between Indians and Mughuls was by no means one-sided, but the Mughuls can indisputably be credited with the introduction of the formal watered oasis garden, a great extension of irrigation, and the custom of building tombs within a garden.

The tomb-building activities of the Mughuls were not Persian, but stemmed from the ancestor veneration of the Mongols, from whom, through Timur Leng, they were descended. Princes and noblemen built their own tombs; during their lifetime the surrounding gardens were used as pleasure grounds but after death were handed over to the priests. These tomb gardens embodied the Muslim ideal of Paradise to be enjoyed by both the living and the dead. In the words of the Qoran:

> With o'erbranching trees in each:
> In each two fountains flowing:
> In each two kinds of every fruit:
> On couches with linings of brocade shall they recline,
>   and the fruit of the two gardens shall be within easy reach:
> Therein shall be the damsels with retiring glances,
>   whom nor man nor djinn hath touched before them:
> Like jacinths and pearls:
> Shall the reward of good be aught but good?
> And beside these shall be two other gardens:
> Of a dark green:
> With gushing fountains in each:
> In each fruits and the palm and the pomegranate:
> In each, the fair, the beauteous ones:
> With large dark eyeballs, kept close in their pavilions:
> Whom man hath never touched, nor any djinn:

*A pool in the Nilkanth pavilion at Mandu,
built by one of Akbar's generals. Jahangir
once picnicked here with his ladies.*

*Their spouses on soft green cushions and on beautiful
carpets shall recline:
Blessed be the name of thy Lord, full of majesty and glory.*

The builders of the tombs would spend whole days with their families and court in the surrounding gardens. This passion for living in the open influenced the design of all their gardens, which were in fact open-air rooms on a lavish scale, where buildings and garden meet, inside and outside, merging imperceptibly into each other. Often gay tents, hung with tapestries, would be pitched on the lawns and just as their camps on the march were laid out as if in a garden, so their gardens served as a form of encampment. The tradition lives on today in the marquees of rugs and tapestries set up for social occasions in the gardens of great houses in India, while open-air living away from the main dwelling is still a feature of Persian life today. The family parties of Iranians picnicking on a summer evening beside the bridge at Isfahan, sitting on flowered rugs to compensate for the vanished flowers of spring, bring to mind the passage in Jahangir's memoirs when he describes the beauties of Shihabur-din-pur in Kashmir: '. . . the whole surface of the ground is grass and trefoil, so much so that to lay a carpet on it would be superfluous and in bad taste.'

The cross-fertilization of ideas with Persia which continued throughout the reigns of the six emperors was stimulated by a renaissance of art which took place in the late sixteenth century in Isfahan. Here Shah Abbas laid out a new capital with gardens and buildings of great magnificence whose beauty can be seen today in the Shah Mosque and other buildings of this period. The close contact between the Mughuls and Persia, their employment of Persian officials and above all their marriages to Persian women, kept traditions alive and constantly renewed. A strong influence was the fact that Persian was the language of the court. It continued to be so even after the fall of the Mughul Empire, eventually becoming the parent of present-day Urdu.

The gardens created by the Mughul dynasty undoubtedly rank as one of the great landscape traditions of the world. Their characteristics are strong and their sense of design impeccable. Water is the connecting theme running throughout, from the source of their inspiration in Persia to the final perfection of the Taj Mahal. Not only the basic form of the design, but every detail is related to the essential life stream of irrigation and to the delight which only water can give. The unity which this obsession gives to the design is so great that, paradoxically, even those gardens from which the water has now been banished are held together by its influence, as by some ghostly presence.

When the Mughuls first came to India their gardens were almost purely Persian, but like all creative artists, they responded to the stimulus of new conditions. The pattern of narrow rills developed into wider canals and great tanks as the Mughuls discovered the joys of cool air generated by the large sheets of water and the need for this in the Indian heat. This development can be traced from the early

Humayun tomb at Delhi where the rills are still narrow, on the Persian pattern, to the Taj Mahal where they have broadened out to eighteen feet.

Another feature which gained importance in a hot climate was the pavilion set within water. This took countless forms, from the simple stone 'thrones' in the water-channels of Nishat and Shalamar to elaborate buildings set in the centre of great tanks and surrounded by spouting jets of water. Another Persian feature which persisted in the early Mughul gardens was the underground room, but as the newcomers adjusted to their surroundings, they delighted more and more in life in the open air. The evolution of the gardens throughout six reigns was towards increasing magnificence and complexity. The level landscape was suited to formal layouts of immense size, while the climate offered a wide choice of trees and flowers, which was continually extended by imports from other regions.

A more generous supply of water constantly inspired designers to new flights of imagination: the single jet from Persian tanks finally developed into hundreds of fountains in Shah Jahan's Shalamar gardens at Lahore, or the artificial rain of Udaipur. Kashmir added a third dimension; the gardens, no longer level, could exploit the possibilities of the mountainside. Nor, in a period of intensely personal rule, can the character of the monarch be discounted. Babur was unusual in that he was absorbed by gardens throughout a turbulent life, since reasonable security is generally essential to garden making. The increasing wealth and power of his successors undoubtedly played a part in design, just as it did in Europe. Above all, skill, imagination and a thorough understanding of the management of water were required, and there was no lack of men with these qualities. Haidar Malik and 'Ali Mardan Khan would have been outstanding engineers in any age.

The planting can only be guessed at from contemporary paintings and memoirs, for it is in this respect that the Mughul gardens have most profoundly changed today, but it was clearly of a luxuriance which needed unlimited supplies of both water and labour for its realization.

If nowadays many of the Mughul gardens of the plain seem more palace than garden, the geometry and sense of enclosure overwhelming, the white marble blinding in the sun, it is because the living elements are missing: water and planting, and the gorgeously caparisoned figures of the Mughuls themselves, with all their animals and birds; for they were not only fine designers, they were also among the greatest of gardeners, and this is vividly portrayed in contemporary miniatures.

In the hot plains of India the Mughuls, who were mountain men, used all their skill to make life bearable in a hot and dusty land. But in Kashmir a new world opened up to them and released a flood of creativity.

The thought of Kashmir had always been a preoccupation of the Mughuls – a promised land. Attempts to annex it were made even during Babur's lifetime and in Humayun's reign Kashmir was for ten years ruled by a cousin, Mirza Muhammad Haidar Dughlat, in the emperor's name, which featured on the coins and in the prayer for the sovereign. Thus, in 1585, when Yusuf Khan, ruler of Kashmir, slackened in his fealty to Akbar, the Mughul emperor sent an army to occupy the country. Not for the first or last time in history the invader considered the occupation to be an act of virtue, but, more unusually, his manifesto was couched in terms of gardens:

'The sole idea of wise kings is day by day to refresh the garden of the world by the streams of justice, and assuredly this design is accomplished whenever extensive countries come into the hands of one who is just and of wide capacity. And when an empire has been civilized by an enlightened and just ruler, and the people thereof – small as well as great – sit in the shade of tranquillity, it is unavoidable that such a prince should cast a profound glance on the deeds of neighbours who have taken the path of dissimulation. He must look closely in order to perceive if their former conduct can be brought into line with love and order, and if they can be induced to treat their subjects properly. If they do not, then justice requires that they should be punished and their land taken from them. . . . Accordingly, when the envoys returned from Kashmir and represented the arrogance and wickedness of the Ruler, H.M. on 20th December 1585 despatched a force.'

The Akbar-nama

This force, although not completely successful, was able to impose a treaty on the Kashmiris, but it was soon broken and in 1586 Akbar dispatched another army with orders to 'practice enlightenment, justice, the non-sufferance of wickedness, the accepting of apologies and the chastisement of the evil'. After stiff fighting in the snowy passes the Mughuls were victorious.

Akbar himself paid a peaceful visit to the country in 1589 but had to return in 1592 to put down another insurrection. He visited Kashmir again in 1597 and on every visit his love for the country grew. From then on successive emperors visited Kashmir and made it their summer home. Their love for it is expressed by Jahangir in his journal:

'Kashmir is a garden of eternal spring, or an iron fort to a palace of kings – a delightful flower-bed, and a heart-expanding heritage for dervishes. Its pleasant meads and enchanting cascades are beyond all description. There are running streams and fountains beyond count. Wherever the eye reaches, there are verdure and running water. The red rose, the violet and the narcissus grow of themselves; in the fields there are all kinds of flowers and all sorts of sweet-scented herbs – more than can be calculated. In the soul-enchanting spring, the hills and the plains are filled with blossom; the gates, the walls, the courts, the roofs are lighted up by the torches of banquet-adorning tulips. What shall we say of these things or of the wide meadows and the fragrant trefoil.

> *The garden nymphs were brilliant,*
> *Their cheeks shone like lamps;*
> *There were fragrant buds on their stems*
> *Like dark amulets on the arms of the beloved.*

The wakeful, ode-rehearsing nightingale
Whetted the desires of wine-drinkers;
At each fountain the duck dipped his beak
Like golden scissors cutting silk;
There were flower carpets and fresh rosebuds,
The wind fanned the lamps of the roses,
The violet braided her locks,
The buds tied a knot in the heart.'

The intense Mughul feeling for Kashmir as a precious and well-guarded jewel echoes the words of their contemporary Shakespeare; 'This other Eden, demi-paradise, this fortress built by Nature for herself'.

Compared to the dry lands where the paradise garden evolved, Kashmir must have appeared as a paradise in itself, a land of fruit, flowers and running water, set within a protective bastion of mountains.

In those days, as now, Kashmir showed the contrast of an intensively cultivated and humanized valley seen against a background of hills rich in native vegetation and rising to the snows. Then, as today, there were great fields of saffron, purple in the autumn, and terraced fields of pale gold rice, their irrigation bunds shaped to the contours of the valley, subtly modelled and blazing in colour like a great canvas by Van Gogh.

Faced with the paradise of Kashmir the remarkable achievement of the Mughuls was that, without losing the strength of their traditional design, they responded to the new conditions. Less imaginative men might have continued to build closely walled gardens on exactly the same pattern as their ancestors. But the Mughuls kept the spirit of their tradition and gave it new dimensions.

The Mughul gardens of Kashmir are perhaps the finest existing example of the adaptation of an established garden tradition to new site conditions. The strength of the mountains as a defence was accepted, the garden walls modified from the complete barrier of the Persian originals to allow landscape and garden to drift into each other. The corner pavilions looking out over the fertile countryside recognize the relaxation of rigid separation between inner paradise and outer desert. These are equivalent to the English gazebos of Tudor times, when it first became desirable to look out from a walled garden into a world growing less hostile.

The skilful adaptation to site is accentuated by the consistent use of traditional elements. The basic form of the *char-bagh* is always there, with straight water-channels crossing at right angles to divide the garden into four quarters. The water-channels are raised so that they will irrigate the sunken parterres of fruit and flowers, and the water is always brimming in the channels. This feature is achieved with great constructional skill and gives an enchantment of reflection, reminiscent of the brimming ablution tanks in the mosque courtyards of Isfahan.

The repeated and varied use of the square gives unity, while there is diversity in the different functions of the garden's parts. The need

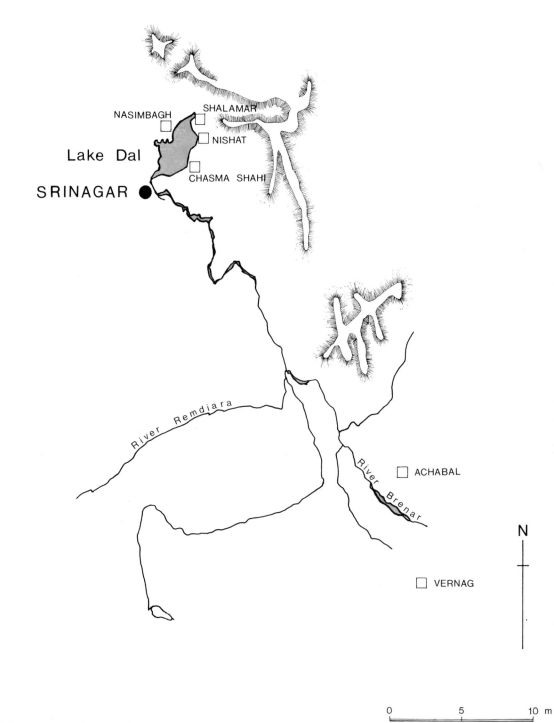

NASIMBAGH

SHALAMAR

NISHAT

Lake Dal

CHASMA SHAHI

SRINAGAR

River Remdiara

ACHABAL

River Brenar

N

VERNAG

0   5   10 m

Map of the surviving gardens in Kashmir.
Peri Mahal, now in ruins and inaccessible, lies
just south-west of Chasma Shahi.

48

for a secluded zenana terrace, unseen from below, yet giving delicious outward views, adds the mystery without which no garden can claim perfection.

A feature of every Kashmir garden and of the landscape of Lake Dal is the heavy solidity of the chenar trees (*Platanus orientalis*). Not only do they give weight, shade and form within the gardens, but their scale is a vital element in relating the gardens to the vast scale of lake and mountain. The solid planting of the peninsula at Nasim Bagh is a magnificently strong element in the lake scene, and it is the chenars which give the unforgettable significance to the Sona Lank island. The suggestion by Archibald Constable that these trees were only introduced in 1632 by 'Ali Mardan Khan suggests that they could have formed no part of the earlier designs. This is hard to believe, and the fact that Jahangir in his memoirs describes a hillside at Safapur in autumn 'with trees of all colours, such as the planes, the apricot and others reflected in the middle of the tank', suggests that they were of a much earlier date. Jahangir also mentions a chenar which, even in Akbar's lifetime, had a hollow trunk large enough to accommodate several armed men. *Platanus orientalis* is a native of Asia Minor and may well have been introduced to Kashmir at a very early date, possibly in the wake of one of those repeated eastward thrusts which swept out of Asia Minor from the days of Darius onwards. The tall slim silhouettes of *Populus italica nigra* which now form so telling a contrast to the broad solid chenars are mentioned by Bernier and were introduced from Italy.

Shalamar Bagh, Kashmir. The avenue of chenars leading from the emperor's private pavilion to the zenana garden. The scale of the trees relates the garden to the surrounding mountains.

49

Panorama of Lake Dal from the Takht-i-Suleiman. In Emperor Jahangir's day the shores of Lake Dal were fringed with gardens. Today, three of these survive, Shalamar Bagh, Nishat Bagh and Chasma Shahi, set in the narrow band of vegetation bordering the lake on the right of the drawing. The ruins of Peri Mahal are perched on the first of the mountain spurs which sweep down to the lake, while Shalamar Bagh is tucked behind the foot of the fourth spur.
The rectangular-shaped land in the centre of the picture is man-made and is given over to market gardening. Srinagar is on the left, with Akbar's fort rising above it on the rocky eminence of Hari Parbat.

COLOUR PLATES
Rice terraces in Kashmir.

Vernag, Kashmir. Innumerable carp swim in the octagonal pool.

Magnificently sited within a total landscape of superb quality, the impact made by the gardens of Kashmir is without parallel, but in studying the whole Mughul tradition they must be seen in relation to the gardens of the plain. The earliest of these pre-date the Kashmir gardens, others are contemporary while some are later. The essential difference is not one of time or of authorship but of site and climate.

To the men from the northern mountains, summer in Kashmir was bliss but life on the hot plains of Agra and Delhi was penance. Babur expressed his despair of Agra as a site for a garden which sounds strangely to us as we look at the glories of his great-great-grandson's Taj, or even when we enjoy the more modest peace of his own Ram Bagh. But this again is a measure of the Mughuls' greatness as garden-makers. When they were given the natural paradise of Kashmir, they responded to the full, but when conditions were not there, they could still create their own paradise.

In the gardens of the hot plains is again seen the walled protection against the outside world which was a feature of the original paradise gardens – a separation from the surrounding landscape, discarded in the kinder land of Kashmir. Yet the feeling for site is still there. The river terraces of the Taj and the Fort at Agra are magnificently conceived, as one looks across from one to the other over the wide bends of the river Jumna.

These gardens of the plain also show a more rigid adherence to the paradise pattern than the freely adapted gardens of Kashmir. The changes of level, the natural setting, which inspired the latter, are replaced by a refinement of design, precious materials and skilled workmanship. They are self-contained and in the main in-looking, except for their views across the river. The gardens in the Forts, at both Delhi and Agra, had to provide for the secluded happiness of the ladies of the Court. Women as strong minded and well loved as Nur Jahan and Mumtaz Mahal could be trusted to ensure that everything possible should be done to make their dwelling a place of delight.

50

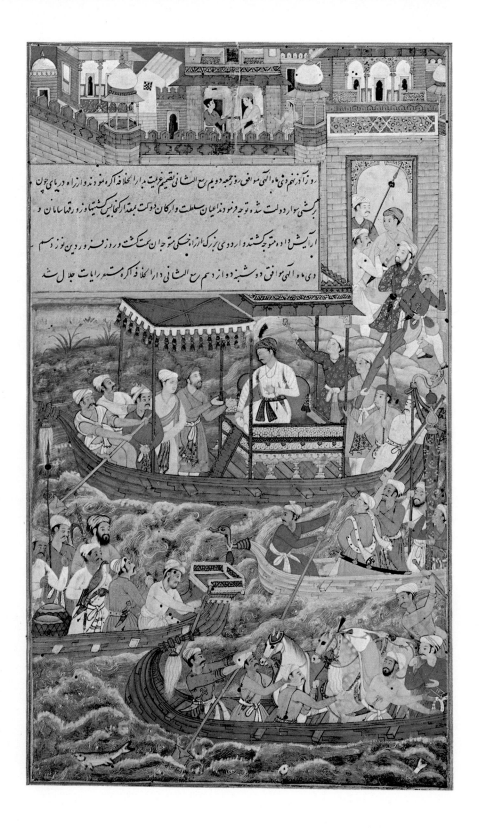

روز آذر نهم وفنى ماه آلهى موافق روز جمعه دويم ربيع الثانى تصميم عزيمت ديار الخلافه آكره نمودند واز راه دريا باى چون

بركشتى سوار دولت شده توجه فرمودند اعيان سلطنت واركان دولت بعد از كنايس كشتيها وزورقها سامان و

آرايش داده متوجه كشتند و اردوى بزرگ از راه خشكى متوجه جان شكستك روز فيروز وروز دين نوزدهم

دى ماه آلهى موافق دوشنبه دوازدهم ربيع الثانى بدار الخلافه آكره مستقر رايات جلال شد

Water, cool breezes, beauty everywhere, views over the river, a certain intricacy within the building complex which gives maximum freedom of movement within confined space, are all here, reminiscent of the courts of the Alhambra built by the Arab conquerors of Spain some two hundred years earlier for a similar purpose and in the same Persian Islamic tradition.

The Mughuls could claim that they understood the very roots of garden design. They combined strength of composition with a feeling for the site, and created their gardens for the pleasure of living, in whatever place and climate they found themselves. They knew how to make the best use of restricted space when necessary, yet could leap the boundaries as effectively as William Kent when opportunity offered. (There is in fact a most skilfully contrived ha-ha in the gardens of Achabal.) Their choice of material and workmanship was superb. They understood and used their native flora, creating gardens which were a reflection of both their way of life and the conditions of their country.

Houseboats near Srinagar. The immediate mountains are gentle, but beyond them stands an encircling ring of snow-covered ranges. The limited land-space between mountain and lake encourages full use of the water margins.

COLOUR PLATE
Akbar leaving Agra by boat, c. 1598.

53

As in all distinctive epochs of art, the Mughul gardens passed from a strong, primitive beginning in Babur's Ram Bagh through the vital and creative phase of Jahangir's Shalamar to the calm perfection of the Taj Mahal, followed by the inevitable decline. But after the creative force of the Mughul garden-makers was spent their influence continued. When Aurangzib finally reversed the religious tolerance initiated by Akbar, and drove the Hindu artists from his court, they were welcomed and employed by the Rajputs, who inherited a part of the Mughul-Persian culture together with the Persian court language. They were wise enough to appreciate the virtues of the formal garden of irrigation in combating the heat of India by the use of wide canals. At Deeg, in 1725, the Rajah of Bharatpur laid out a garden embodying the paradise tradition as adapted to the hot land of Hind. So well attuned to the Indian climate and way of life is this tradition that one may hope to see it undergo a new renaissance.

The years between Babur's invasion of the Punjab in 1520 and the deposition of Shah Jahan in 1658 roughly span the finest age of the Mughul gardens which, curiously, coincides with great epochs of garden-making in other parts of the world. Villa Lante, representing the height of the Italian Renaissance gardens, was built in 1564, during Akbar's reign, and Le Nôtre began his great garden at Vaux-le-Vicomte, in 1658, four years after the completion of the Taj Mahal. In England Montacute is representative of seventeenth-century gardens and its gazebos recall those in Kashmir. In the Far East also, the sixteenth and seventeenth centuries saw the greatest period of the Japanese tradition, which culminated in the perfection of the Katsura Imperial Villa at Kyoto.

Each of these expressions of the garden ideal evolved from the individual characteristics of the people who made them and of the lands in which they arose. Yet the strands of which these diverse garden traditions were woven had often crossed each other in the course of history, and sometimes the original inspiration sprang from the same source but grew in different directions.

Inspiration born of the pattern of irrigation is evident in the Italian gardens, and to a less extent in the French, while a simple form of the paradise garden appeared in the medieval gardens of France and England.

Superficially, the Mughul gardens show a considerable resemblance to those of the Italian Renaissance, but there are fundamental differences. The starting-point of the Italian garden is the house, from which the garden extends out into the landscape. The Mughul garden on the other hand is a dwelling-place in its own right, not necessarily connected with a house or palace. In Kashmir it is the surrounding landscape which is the dominating factor and which is drawn inwards to the heart of the garden rather than the garden pressing out into the landscape. While the use of water as a central theme is shared by Mughuls and Italians, their attitude to it is quite different. The Mughul relies on the form and quality of the water itself, keeping that which contains it simple. In Italian gardens, the water gushes from carved figures and flows into wrought basins but the intricate carving of the *chadar* in the Mughul garden is designed not to be seen itself but to give shape to the falling water. In Italy a torch is likely to be held aloft by a carved Titan, in India the lamps are housed in sconces hidden by the falling water through which the light will shine.

This difference is partly accounted for by the Muslims' religious objection to the representation of living creatures, but it also reflects the greater joy and veneration for water felt by the Mughuls.

There is little common ground between the French and Mughul gardens except that they both served as settings for court ceremonial, with the difference that the Mughul gardens also provided places for seclusion and informal living. The transformation of Lutyens' 'Mughul' garden in Delhi when it is functioning ceremonially, with red-uniformed guards forming avenues down the walks and standing at focal points to illumine the design, gives an idea of the added richness which court functions must have conferred, especially on the larger and more formal gardens.

The only similarity between the Mughul garden-makers and their contemporaries in Japan is that both loved plants and respected nature, and were strongly influenced by religion. But whereas Japanese Zen Buddhism worked through the sanctity of living forms, the Muslim religion stressed geometric form.

The Japanese garden owed distant inspiration to the Buddhist temple gardens which had travelled east from India, long before the Mughuls' day. This well illustrates the complex interweaving of ideas and the cross-fertilization between cultures of different lands and ages. The seeds of thought are passed constantly from one nation to another, and when they germinate into some great art, the form it takes is dictated by the time, the place and the people.

Of all the great gardens of the world, those nearest to the Mughuls' in form and feeling are the Hispano-Arabic gardens of the Alhambra and Generalife and this suggests that the Persian/Muslim influences were for the Mughuls the strongest of all, whatever other strands were intermingled.

Today, some of the great water gardens of the Indian subcontinent are mere shadows of their former selves. The causes are many: time, war, pillage, neglect, thoughtless development. The Shalamar gardens at Delhi have all but vanished, the water-palace of Peri Mahal lies in ruins on its hillside above Lake Dal, Aurangzib's daughter and her gardens are both forgotten. Yet many are still well maintained, and the restoration of both buildings and parterres has been of a very high order. In some, the water is of necessity diverted to the more pressing needs of food production. Even so, the diversion is often only temporary. The fortunate visitor may find the fountains playing, so that prospect and sound, together with the joy of cool air in the heat, delight all the senses together, just as their original designers intended.

BABUR 1508-1530

Bagh-i-wafa, Kabul, Afghanistan

Ram Bagh, Agra

Babur, who was to become the first Mughul emperor, counted both Jenghis Khan and Timur Leng among his ancestors. A son of the king of Ferghana, a little mountain kingdom east of Samarkand, his life was one of constant warfare, movement, and alternating victory and defeat. Yet through it all, he remained deeply influenced by his love of nature, the memory of his early homes in Ferghana and Kabul, and by the great impression made on him in his youth by the splendours of Herat and Samarkand.

Succeeding to the throne of Ferghana at the age of eleven, Babur was soon, nominally at least, at the head of his armies, and at fourteen, for a brief period, he captured Samarkand. There followed seven years of the ebb and flow of war and fortune, until, within four months of leaving his homeland of Ferghana as a fugitive, he became king of Kabul. There his son Humayun was born; a great feast was held to celebrate the birth, and soon after, to raise the standing of his little kingdom, and as a ruler descended from Timur Leng, he assumed the title of Padshah or Emperor.

Now, to improve his new kingdom, and with Samarkand always in his mind, he began to lay out gardens. His favourite, the Bagh-i-wafa, the Garden of Fidelity, is described in his memoirs. There were others, such as the garden at Istalif which he bought from its owners, and refashioned to his own ideas of what was orderly and beautiful. Vigne, visiting Kabul in the middle of the nineteenth century found plane trees of Babur's planting still flourishing at his favourite drinking-place, Khoja-seh-Yeran on the Kabul-Kohista road.

It was from Kabul that he launched his invasions of India, less it would seem from choice than from sheer necessity, since Kabul could not provide the resources necessary to keep his troops provisioned and the riches of Hindustan were legendary. Once established in Agra, Babur and his men clearly found the heat and humidity of India trying. He complains of dust and particularly of hot winds and regards it as a matter of urgent necessity to develop a new environment, to keep his followers reasonably contented. In this water was to play an important part; whether in the garden, in pools, channels and fountains, or indoors in the form of baths.

'One of the great defects of Hindustan being its lack of running waters, it kept coming to my mind that waters should be made to flow by means of wheels erected wherever I might settle down, also that grounds should be laid out in an orderly and symmetrical way.'

Water-colour of a water-wheel. Babur commented with some asperity upon the relative hygiene of the Lahore and Agra methods of operating water-wheels.

Miniature of Babur supervising the making of his favourite garden, the Bagh-i-wafa, or Garden of Fidelity. The exact location of the garden is uncertain. For climatic reasons it is unlikely to have been in or near Kabul itself, but at a lower altitude. At Nimla, near Jelalabad, some 5,000 feet lower down on the Kabul river, are the remains of an unidentified Mughul garden.

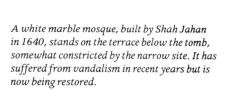

A white marble mosque, built by Shah Jahan in 1640, stands on the terrace below the tomb, somewhat constricted by the narrow site. It has suffered from vandalism in recent years but is now being restored.

Within days of reaching a decision, work would be begun. At least three great gardens in Agra are attributed to Babur himself: Ram Bagh, Dehra Bagh and Zahara Bagh, the two latter being for his daughters. Buildings of all kinds were included in the garden-palaces, together with wells, reservoirs, aqueducts and bath-houses, the latter being provided with hot water. One remarkable enterprise was a well containing a three-storeyed house: 'When the water is at its lowest, it is one step below the bottom chamber; when it rises in the Rains, it sometimes goes into the top storey'. Thus in the hottest weather, descent to the lowest floor could offer water and a cool atmosphere.

His followers profited by his example: 'Khalifa also and Shaikh Zain, Hunas-il 'ali and whoever got land on that other bank of the river laid out regular and orderly gardens with tanks, made running waters also by setting up wheels like those in Dipalpur and Lahore.'

Apart from these sites there is evidence of gardens, palaces and wells extending along the whole east bank of the Jumna river, and inland to Nunhai, and it seems clear that the whole area was the stretch of ground which 'the people of Hind, who had never seen grounds planned so symmetrically and thus laid out, called the side of the Jun where (our) residences were, Kabul.' There is scope for further excavation here before all traces of the past are lost.

The founder of the Mughul Empire was probably also its most attractive character. Capable, like all his successors, of cruelties, he was nevertheless by the standards of his time a humane and civilized man. He restrained the worst excesses of his troops, he built and planted as well as destroyed, he held feasts, wrote verse, spoke both Turki and Persian, and has left in his memoirs a detailed picture not only of his campaigns but of his own enjoyment of life in its fullest sense. Time and again he refers to the sheer physical joy he experienced, often at periods of extreme danger, in having surmounted his difficulties. He had the gift, too, of retaining the loyalty of his followers, rare at a time when it was considered no disgrace to sell allegiance to the highest bidder.

When the demands of war allowed it, he was always ready to enjoy his pleasures: hunting, drinking-parties with his friends, and above all his gardens. Once at least, exasperated by intrigues, he threatened to retire and to live like a hermit in his 'Gold-scattering garden' at Agra.

Babur's tomb, Kabul.
Babur directed that his grave should be 'open to the sky, with no building over it, no need of a door-keeper'. To preserve the tomb, however, an open modern structure has now been built over it. A garden with four terraces surrounds the tomb, which is on the topmost terrace but one. Beside it is the tomb of Babur's youngest son, Hindal; on the top terrace Hindal's daughter lies buried. Judas trees flank the central path and steps, at the bottom of which stands a huge chenar. *But the terraces are neglected and overgrown with weeds and wild flowers such as henbane and campanulas.*

He combined two essential qualities for the gardener, a natural affinity with plants and a dedicated attention to detail. When finally settled to his life in India he still found time to write to his Governor in Kabul, Khvaja Kilan, with instructions that the gardens he had planted there should be kept well watered and properly maintained with flowers. Whatever the matter in hand, whether comparing different ways of raising water from a well, choosing oleanders for their colours, or arranging for the import of fruit trees, he brought to the project the same *élan* and commitment that gave him his victories in battle.

His heart was in Kabul. He left explicit directions in his will as to his burial place. A terraced garden on the slopes of the hill Shah-i-Kabul, it looks out over the plains and towards the snows and the hills which had been his hunting-grounds.

BAGH-I-WAFA, KABUL, AFGHANISTAN
'I laid out the Four-gardens, known as the Bagh-i-wafa, on a rising ground, facing south. . . . There oranges, citrons and pomegranates grow in abundance . . . I had plantains brought and planted there; they did very well. The year before, I had had sugar-cane planted there; it also did well. . . . The garden lies high, has running water close at hand, and a mild winter climate. In the middle of it, a one-mill stream flows constantly past the little hill on which are the four garden-plots. In the south-west part of it there is a reservoir 10 by 10, round which are orange trees and a few pomegranates, the whole encircled by a trefoil meadow. This is the best part of the garden, a most beautiful sight when the oranges take colour. Truly that garden is admirably situated.'

Once, resting there upon his way to a campaign, he wrote:

'Next day I went to the Bagh-i-wafa. Those were the days of the

'The Emperor Baber's tomb is close to the city . . . it is surrounded by a large garden, the underwood of which is formed by bushes of the Alu-balu, *or wild cherry, which here as well as in Kabul is planted for the sake of its white blossoms.'* G. T. VIGNE, 1850

garden's beauty; its lawns were one sheet of trefoil, its pomegranate trees yellowed to autumn splendour, their fruit full red; fruit on the orange trees green and glad, countless oranges but not yet as yellow as our hearts desired. . . . The one excellent and blessed content we have had from the Bagh-i-wafa was had at this time.'

It is perhaps the greatest felicity that the landscape designer knows: to design a garden; to be forced by circumstance to be absent for some years, and then to return, to find, as if by magic, time elided, and his creation come, overnight, to maturity and splendour, just as he had first imagined it.

RAM BAGH, AGRA

Babur's description of the first garden he laid out on the banks of the Jumna River is a classic of the transformation of an unfavourable site.

'With this object in view, we crossed the Jun-water (Jumna) to look at garden-grounds a few days after entering Agra. Those grounds were so bad and unattractive that we traversed them with a hundred disgusts and repulsions. So ugly and displeasing were they, that the idea of making a Char-bagh in them passed from my mind, but needs must! As there was no other land near Agra, that same ground was taken in hand a few days later.

The beginning was made with the large well from which water comes for the Hot bath, and also with the piece of ground where the tamarind trees and the octagonal tank now are. After that came the large tank, with its enclosure; after that the tank and *talar* [the *talar* is raised on pillars and open in front; it serves often for an audience hall] in front of the outer residence; after that the private house with its garden and various dwellings; after that the Hot bath. Then in that charmless and disorderly Hind, plots of garden were seen laid out with order and symmetry, with suitable borders and parterres in every corner and in every border rose and narcissus in perfect arrangement.'

There have been many speculations as to the site of Babur's first Agra garden. There is evidence that he built a garden-palace at the bend of the river, looking southwards across it, and that this was later completed by his son Humayun. Traditionally, this site has been known as the Chahar Bagh, and traces of a number of wells and buildings have been found. The Zahara Bagh too, built for Babur's daughter Zahara, has some claim to be the original. This was one of the largest garden-palaces in Agra, lying between the Ram Bagh and the site of the Chini-ka-Roza. The great octagonal well here apparently survived until about 1912.

The probability however is that the real site is that of the Ram Bagh, originally the Aram Bagh or Garden of Rest. Also known as the Nur Afshan, it is almost certainly the earliest Mughul garden to survive in recognizable form, although much altered since. It could indeed be described as 'orderly and symmetrical'. The basic pattern is one of geometrically laid-out walks, with platforms raised well above ground-level from which to view the garden. A terrace follows the east bank of the Jumna, and on it are the remains of two substantial buildings. Towards the south, a fine aqueduct and well

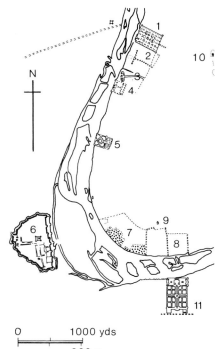

Plan of Agra: the principal Mughul gardens were sited along the banks of the Jumna, and particularly along its eastern curve.
Key: (1) Ram Bagh (2) Zahara Bagh (3) Chini-ka-Roza (4) Wazir Khan ka Bagh (5) Tomb of I'timad-ud-Daula (6) Agra Fort (7) Chahar Bagh (8) Mehtab Khan ka Bagh (9) Humayun's mosque (10) Nunhai village (11) Taj Mahal.

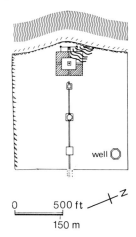

Remains of Zahara Bagh, Agra, made by Babur for his daughter.

63

Above: *Ram Bagh, Agra. The narrow water-courses of the early Mughul gardens derive from Persian irrigation, where in the wealthier properties the channels bringing water from the fields were lined with dressed stone or tiles. Trees were planted in the square openings.*

Above right: *From the well in the background water is brought to the garden by a canal, built on arches to allow irrigation of the ground at a lower level. In the foreground is a patterned* chadar, *or chute, down which water ripples from one level to another.*

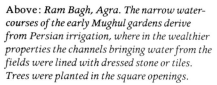

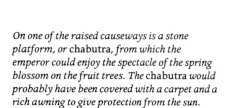

On one of the raised causeways is a stone platform, or chabutra, *from which the emperor could enjoy the spectacle of the spring blossom on the fruit trees. The* chabutra *would probably have been covered with a carpet and a rich awning to give protection from the sun.*

Ram Bagh. Pavilions overlooking the river Jumna. This was part of the area known to the local population as 'Kabul' and there must once have been many such pavilions lining the eastern bank of the river.

survive in a good state of preservation, while the waterchannels throughout are seen in their earliest and purest form, mere runnels to irrigate the roots of trees. A circular gravel space also indicates what may have been the site of Babur's original octagonal well.

The structures remain, the planting has been much altered. Part of the site is now in use as a nursery garden and this seems closer to the spirit of the original than the later forest trees. At first sight, one seems lost in winding groves. Yet, once mounted to the platforms, it is still possible to appreciate the special relationship of the garden with the sky, and the rapidly changing Indian light. From these platforms, too, the Mughuls would have found it possible to look down upon the fruit and flowers of the original plantings, seated in spring above a floor of blossom. Little visited today, but alive with birds and animals – vultures, green parakeets and monkeys – Ram Bagh is of unique historical interest as the forerunner of the whole glittering series of Mughul gardens. Babur is said to have been buried here temporarily before his body was taken to his garden at Kabul.

The Ram Bagh was evidently well maintained in his great-grandson's reign, for Jahangir writes:

'On this day I went round to see the Garden of Gul-Afshan [Babur's] which is on the banks of the Jumna. On the way rain fell heavily and filled the mead with freshness and greenness. Pineapples had arrived at perfection, and I made a thorough inspection. Of the buildings that overlooked the river, none that I saw were without the charm of verdure and flowing water.'

'On Wednesday, together with the ladies seated in a boat, I went to the Nur-Afshan Garden and rested there at night. As the garden belongs to the establishment of Nur Jahan B., on Thursday the 4th she held the royal entertainment [in celebration of the commencement of the 16th year of the reign] and presented great offerings.'

A young prince (possibly Shah Jahan in his youth, or Shah Suja) drinking in a garden attended by a number of learned men, one of whom is playing the vina. *In the background, on a white marble platform under a canopy, is spread the prince's couch. By Bichitr, from a royal album once in the possession of the Emperors Jahangir and Shah Jahan, mainly executed between 1605 and 1658.*

HUMAYUN 1530-1556

'I have seen few persons possessed of so much natural talent and excellence as he, but in consequence of frequent intercourse with the sensual and profligate men who served him . . . he had contracted some bad habits; among these was his addiction to opium. All the evil that has been set down to the Emperor, and has become the common talk of the people, is attributable to this vice. Nevertheless, he was endowed with excellent qualities, being brave in battle, gay in feast and very generous. In short, he was a dignified, stately and regal sovereign, who observed much state and pomp.'

The *Tarikh-i-Rashidi*, by Mirza Muhammad Haidar Dughlat, a cousin of Babur

Of the six remarkable men who succeeded one another in direct line as Mughul emperors, Humayun was the weakest link. Born in 1508, within ten years of his accession, he had lost almost all Babur's empire, and was in flight from his enemies at the time of his son's birth. Crossing into Persia, he appealed to Shah Tahmasp for help. Here he was generously received, indeed fêted, and in due course provided with fresh troops. Eventually, after various campaigns, he recovered his losses, finally entering Delhi once again as emperor.

A mixture of courage and indolence, he failed to exploit his successes in battle and threw away his opportunities, to indulge instead in long bouts of feasting and drinking or in his greatest interests, dress and ceremonial.

His half-sister, Gulbadan Begam, describes his amusements in detail in the *Humayun-nama*. On the river bank at Agra he set up the House of Feasting, or Mystic House. The design shows the Mughul preoccupation with octagons which was to be expressed in his tomb and later, with even greater distinction, in the Taj Mahal. The principal room was octagonal; within it was set an octagonal water-tank and, in the centre of this, a platform of the same shape, spread with Persian carpets. On the platform sat graceful and decorative young men and girls, together with musicians. Boats, too, were decorated, possibly to sail on the tank, one even having a garden, with 'amaranthus and cockscombs and larkspur'.

Here, says Gulbadan, the fancy once took him to say to his hostess '"Dearest lady, if you approved, they might put water in the tank". She replied: "Very good" and went herself and sat at the top of the steps. People were taking no notice, when all at once the tap was turned and water came. The young people got very much excited. His Majesty said: "There is no harm; each of you will eat a

Miniature of the Feast of the Birth of Humayun (Mughul, c. 1590). The classic features of Mughul design, the square tank with fountains, the water-courses, the stone chabutra, *provide the setting for the life and growth and vitality in which these gardens once abounded. The rich carpet echoes the spring flowers, the chenar, the cypress and canopy provide shade; and while the musicians, dancer and juggler entertain him the emperor inspects his presents.*

pellet of anise and a bit of comfit [to prevent a chill] and come out of there.'' Upon this everyone who would eat the comfit came out quickly. The water was as high as their ankles. To end the story, everyone ate the comfit [*ma'jùn*] and all came out.' Here, evidently, was a prototype of that classic garden conceit, the water joke, evoking comparisons as far apart as Hellbrunn in Austria and Wilton House, Salisbury, where at one time visitors examining statuary in a grotto were suddenly drenched in water. More than the comfits were provided for the young people in the tank: they received a generous share of gifts and ceremonial robes.

Jewelled thrones, with golden hangings and strings of pearls provided the setting. Feasts on a splendid scale were held, together with the giving and receiving of presents. This latter custom, to Indians a traditional ceremony, was often misunderstood by Europeans, who supposed it to be in the nature of a bribe. Much later, Tavernier, a French jeweller in India during the reign of Shah Jahan, wrote:

'Whoever he be that crave Audience of the King, they ask him in the first place, where the Present is which he intends for the King; and examine whether it be fitting to present to his Majesty. For no man must come into his presence empty-handed, though it be an honour dearly purchas'd.'

Elsewhere in the palace were the Houses of Dominion, Good Fortune and Pleasure, devoted respectively to the arts of war, literature and love.

Ritual was all-important. The emperor set up seven halls of audience, named after the seven planets, and would only transact business appropriate to the day of the planet. Sundays and Tuesdays, the days of the Sun and Mars, were for affairs of State; Mondays and Wednesdays for pleasure, while Friday was for councils and assemblies.

All this reveals yet another aspect of the Mughul passion for order, symmetry and a mystic relationship with numbers. It is in complete contrast to the Hindu art of the conquered territories, with its organic character and intricate rendering of natural form. When Babur visited Gwalior, with its temples and palaces, he was so shocked at their nature that he ordered some of the sculpture to be destroyed.

Humayun evidently completed and lived in one of Babur's garden-palaces at Agra, but he was himself comparatively un-interested in gardens. Although from time to time he visited his orange gardens, making long journeys to the mountain passes to do so, he had none of the passionate interest in horticulture which distinguished his father and his grandson.

He is commemorated in his tomb at Delhi, perhaps more splendidly than the facts warrant. He had entered the city as a conqueror in July 1555. Six months later, almost to the day, while descending from the roof of the Sher Mandal in Delhi, he heard the muezzin sound the call to prayer. Stopping immediately, he knelt upon the stairs. As he rose his staff slipped. He became entangled in his robe and fell, receiving injuries from which he died a few days later.

HUMAYUN'S TOMB, DELHI

This was one of the first garden tombs, of which the Mughul period produced so many splendid examples, and is Humayun's great memorial (begun *c.* 1560, completed 1573).

These, in their owner's lifetime, following Tartar and Mongol tradition, were places of resort and pleasure, and nobles, as well as those of royal blood, tried to outdo one another in their magnificence. At death, the central pavilion became the mausoleum and the site was handed over to the care of holy men. This was perhaps not wholly unconnected with the fiscal system which presently developed under Akbar and which amounted to a completely confiscatory death duty. The wealthy therefore spent in their lifetime what otherwise at death would pass to the emperor.

Built by his widow, Haji Begam, Humayun's tomb is a remarkable example of that contrast of red sandstone and white marble which

Humayun's tomb seen from the back. The tomb is built of Tantpura red sandstone, with dressings of white Makrana marble.

Humayun's tomb: a large well attached to the north gateway provided a head of water for the garden.

Below: *one of the intersections.*

'The four main parterres are subdivided by minor causeways into smaller plots (32 in all). The crossings of these causeways are emphasized by shallow tanks and platforms, and at each fall of the ground level the channels are provided with scalloped red sandstone chutes.' ARCHAEOLOGICAL SURVEY OF INDIA

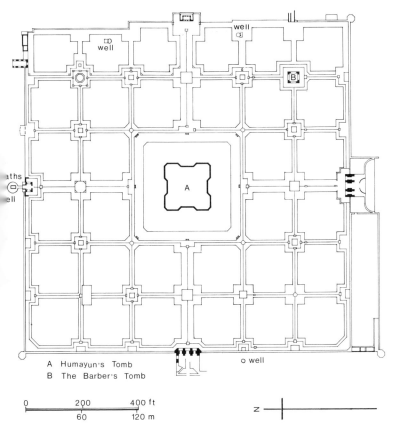

A Humayun's Tomb
B The Barber's Tomb

```
0        200        400 ft
|---------|----------|
    60         120 m
```

z ──┼──

*Plan of Humayun's tomb. 'The garden is a
purely Persian feature and is the earliest extant
Mughal garden in India still preserving its
original form. The causeways, 41' 6" in width,
are provided with narrow water channels in
the centre . . . the ancestors of the broad canals
characteristic of the later Mughal gardens.'*
ARCHAEOLOGICAL SURVEY OF INDIA

was to become a recurrent theme. The surrounding layout was
probably begun in his lifetime and it is the earliest Mughul garden
plan known to survive without alteration. A parterre rather than a
garden, it takes the *char-bagh* motive and enlarges and repeats it in an
intricate pattern, almost wholly two-dimensional and strongly Persian
in character. The channels and tanks have the depth of mere engravings, but minute differences of level are created in order to exploit
the ripple of water, which was lifted from great wells outside the
garden.

The parterre is in a good state of restoration, although the flowers,
most of the trees and above all water itself which once decorated
it are lacking. But the plan is on an impressive scale, and it is arguable
that its simplicity sets off, better than any planting, the tomb itself, a
mass of glowing complicated colour on its monumental quartzite
platform.

AKBAR 1556-1605

Hari Parbat and Nasim Bagh, Kashmir

Akbar's Tomb, Sikandra

Akbar's empire at his death in 1605.
On his accession in 1556 Akbar's actual
possessions were limited to a few districts of
the Punjab, although he had received pledges of
loyalty from chiefs in certain other parts of the
Punjab and from the Governor of Delhi. In the
49 years of his reign his empire grew to reach
across more than half India. His first
conquests extended it up to the wall of the
Himalayas, from the borders of Kashmir
south-eastwards to Allahabad. Finally it
stretched from Baluchistan and Kashmir in
the north-west to the Deccan in the south, and
to the Indian Ocean in the Bay of Bengal.

Opposite:
Fatehpur Sikri. Miniature of the birth of
Prince Murad at Fatehpur Sikri. In a room on
the right, astrologers are seen casting the
child's horoscope.

The great Akbar was born at what must have seemed an inauspicious moment, when his father, stripped of all his possessions, was temporarily a refugee in the little principality of Umarkhot. Yet it is said that when Humayun saw his son's horoscope, he leaped with joy. The years were indeed to justify such a prophecy.

In Akbar the Mughul Empire found, for the first time, a man able to weld the gains resulting from his conquests into a unified and viable whole, so that his successors were in a position to administer, to consolidate and to cultivate the arts, secure in the knowledge that their achievements would not disintegrate behind them each time they were called away to some rebellious province. In some part this was due to the sound and practical government already established in the east by Humayun's great adversary, Sher Khan, but primarily to Akbar's personal qualities of greatness. Unable throughout his life to read and write, and as a young man almost exclusively occupied in sport, he combined courage and statesmanship with a religious and racial tolerance hitherto unknown. As part of his policy of conciliation, he married a princess of Jaipur, Jodh Bai, who became the mother of Jahangir, and he took Hindus into his service in many capacities. In architecture, especially, their contribution was a notable one, giving the buildings their own vivid Mughul-Rajput character.

Two great projects of his time were the city of Fatehpur Sikri and the Fort at Agra. The former, a city of palaces and gardens, was built at the shrine of Sheikh Salim, who had foretold the birth of his sons, and where his son Prince Salim, afterwards the Emperor Jahangir, was born. A walled city, with an artificial lake to the north-west, it was provided with a complex system of reservoirs and Persian wheels for the supply of water. It had already fallen into ruins in Akbar's lifetime, when he moved his court elsewhere, but part has since been carefully restored. Various reasons have been put forward for its desertion; that the situation was unhealthy, or that the water supply was inadequate. It is said that the dam of the lake actually gave way while the Emperor and his friends were playing cards on the bank, and the party narrowly escaped drowning.

At Agra, much of Akbar's work in the great city fort was replaced by his grandson, Shah Jahan, but the magnificent walls remain intact to the present day. A builder rather than a gardener he had, nevertheless, some hand in the making of gardens, and had trees and

Hari Parbat, Srinagar. Akbar's fort, seen across lotus leaves.

flowers of all kinds imported and planted at Agra and Fatehpur Sikri. A description survives of one of his Agra gardens:

'The Gardens about Agra are many, but the cheifest are Darree ca baug (Dehra Bagh) and King Ecbars on this side the river, and Mootee ca Baag on the otherside, the latter built by Nooremohol . . . In some, little groves of trees, as Apple trees (those scarse), Orenge Trees, Mulberrie trees etts. mango trees, Caco (cocoanut) trees, Figg trees, Plantan trees (bananas), theis latter in rancks, as are the Cipresse trees. In other squares are your flowers, herbes, etts., whereof Roses, Marigolds (theis scarse only in Mootee ca Baag) to be seen; French Marigolds aboundance; Poppeas redd, carnation and white; and divers other sortes of faire flowers which we knowe not in our parts, many groweing on prettie trees, all watered by hand in tyme of drought, which is 9 moneths in the yeare.'

The Travels of Peter Mundy

More significant, however, in its effect on the art of garden design was Akbar's conquest of Kashmir. At their first attempt in 1585 the Mughul forces were unable to penetrate much beyond the borders of Kashmir, largely because they underestimated the difficulties – cold, snow, and the scarcity of provisions. They were forced to agree to a compromise peace: Yusuf Khan should remain the Ruler of Kashmir, while Akbar figured upon the coins and in the official prayers.

Opposite: Akbar, in an elephant fight, pursues his rival across a bridge of boats.

Fatehpur Sikri. The Turkish sultana's house with the chaman *tank in the foreground.*

Opposite:
A royal progress on Lake Wular, Kashmir. The inscription above the emperor's head reads 'Akbar', but the features are those of Jahangir. When Akbar visited Kashmir, Abu-'l-Fazl wrote: 'As in this country there were more than 30,000 boats but none fit for the world's lord, able artificers soon prepared river palaces, and made flower gardens on the surface of the water.'

Saffron, always an important crop in Kashmir, was to be the emperor's.

Soon, however, the Kashmiris, feeling themselves secure in their ring of mountains, were slipping back into their old ways:

'H.M. addressed himself anew to the conquest of the country . . . a meeting of astrologers was held, and a close investigation of the horoscope of the year and of the state of the constellations was made. The diagrams showed that if some energy was exerted the conquest would be quickly made.'

This time the campaign was pursued in earnest. A large force was despatched through Bhimbar and Rajauri, and after snowstorms and bitter fighting in the passes, the Mughul armies finally won a decisive battle in October 1586. Three years later, Akbar set out to visit Kashmir for the first time, taking the route through Bhimbar and the Pir Panjal passes. The whole journey from Lahore to Srinagar took about six weeks and was made in summer. Five thousand men in all, labourers, stone-cutters and miners, were sent off in advance to improve the road and, in spite of deep snow on the passes, the crossing was safely accomplished.

Once arrived, the emperor could enjoy to the full the delights Kashmir has to offer. River palaces, floating gardens and more than a thousand boats were prepared in his honour and he made what must have been a splendid progress on the water. This was in a tradition which survives to the present day, for many of the Lake Dal houseboats carry gardens, and considerable crops, such as melons and tomatoes, are grown on the floating islands.

The Imperial tents. These show a remarkable affinity with the mosques and madressehs of Isfahan. Drawings by H. Blochmann

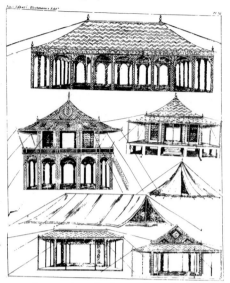

Top, the Bargah. *Left, the* Duashyanah Manzil *or two-storeyed house. It was at the window of this that the emperor showed himself to his Court each morning. Right centre, top, a* Chobin Rawati, *typical of the harem tents.*

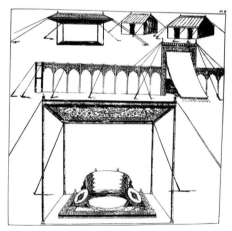

Top row, various tents. Centre, the Sarapardah *and* Gulbadar *floored with carpets. Below, the* Namgirah, *or dew catcher, with carpet and pillow. Here the emperor sat in the evening and only those highest in his favour were admitted to his presence.*

In all, Akbar visited Kashmir three times. He seems especially to have enjoyed the autumn colour and the saffron fields, and visited the spring at Achabal, already a place of pilgrimage. He found a richly fertile country, with abundant sunshine. The clear cut progression of seasons: spring with its wealth of flowers, the generously productive summer, the blazing trees of autumn and the sparkling snow scenes of winter: all combined to make of Kashmir what Akbar once called his private garden. To this was now added the genius of men and women with a passion for the making of gardens, and with wealth and power at their disposal to carry out their wishes.

The journeys of the Imperial Court to Kashmir are celebrated, and at the halting-places which became established on those journeys, gardens were laid out: Wah Bagh, Rajauri and many others lie along the route, comparatively little visited today and some in ruins. But it was above all at Srinagar, the natural heart of Kashmir, the objective of the journeys, that the finest gardens came into being. Lake Dal, with its ring of mountains, in snow from October to May, the two hills of Hari Parbat and Takht-i-Suleiman rising dramatically from its shore, the bunds and islands of earlier provenance, offered an almost unlimited choice of splendid sites. All round the lake shore are traces of old Mughul gardens, while the map is littered with their names. A count taken in Jahangir's time showed over seven hundred of them. Akbar's own contributions to Lake Dal were the fortress of Hari Parbat and the garden-palace of Nasim Bagh.

In a life of movement, it is not surprising to learn that the emperor devoted a good deal of thought to the comfort and organization of journeys, whether for pleasure, or with his troops. Once again, the ruling passion was for order, and some of these temporary encampments must have been of surprising beauty. Men and material in vast quantities would be sent off to prepare the site in advance, and the site itself would be carefully chosen to be agreeable. We read of a hundred elephants, five hundred camels, five hundred escorting troopers, and nearly two thousand men employed in all capacities to set up the camps.

First there would be a large enclosure, capable of being locked, with at one end a pavilion for worship and for morning greetings, for it was essential that the emperor should show himself daily to his subjects. Next came apartments for the harem and tents for the servants. Beyond this was a succession of open spaces and enclosures, all to prescribed dimensions, culminating in the grand hall, which might be floored with as many as a thousand carpets, where the Imperial audiences were held. The materials were sumptuous, brocades, velvets and embroideries, protected by awnings of canvas and waxcloth. Over it all was set a great lantern, the Akas Diya, some forty yards high and guyed with sixteen ropes, to illuminate the camp from afar. Engravings show that these temporary buildings have a strong link with Persian designs; they might almost be a stage equivalent of the real thing: mosques, arcades and pavilions of all kinds. The Shah of Persia's tents at the 1971 Persepolis celebrations were in the same tradition.

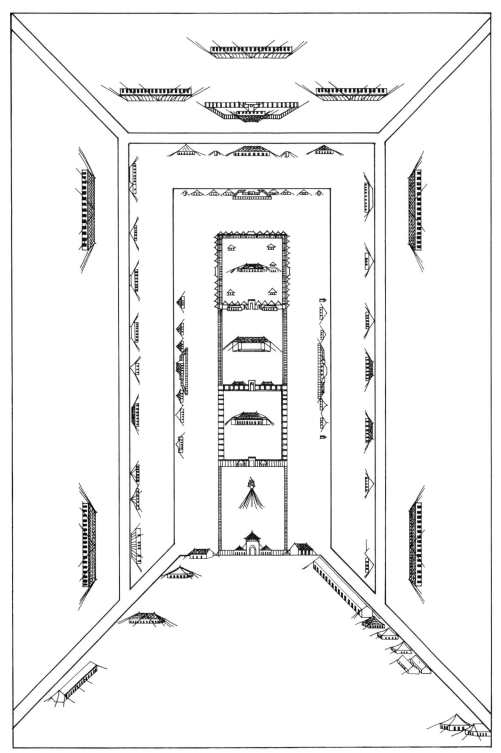

Plan of tents, showing how the emperor's camp was arranged.

The Friday Mosque, Isfahan.

There seemed no limit to Akbar's energy and inventiveness. He ordered the translation of Babur's memoirs from Turki into Persian, and engaged the finest artists of the day to illustrate it; he collected a huge library; although unable himself to read, tutors expounded the books to him, while writers waited at hand to take down his own words. It is also thanks to him that we have such a detailed and lively picture of his own times. He commissioned from the Persian Abu-'l-Fazl both the *Akbar-nama*, a history of his reign, and the *Ain-i-Akbari*, covering every aspect of life from court ceremonial to weights and measures. He designed illuminations; he engaged throughout his life in sport of every kind to the point of recklessness, from water-fowling to polo and elephant-fighting. All this was peripheral to a lifetime devoted increasingly to the business of government: we are told that he devoted sixteen hours a day to state affairs. A clue to it all is perhaps given by his biographer in the *Ain-i-Akbari:* 'the Emperor never wasted a moment of his time. . . .'

On the 15th of October 1605 Akbar died in the fortress at Agra. He was buried just outside the city at Sikandra, where the South Gate bears the inscription:

'These are the gardens of Eden, enter them to live for ever.'

HARI PARBAT AND NASIM BAGH, KASHMIR

Akbar's fortress of Hari Parbat dominates Srinagar and the lake. As it exists today, probably only the outer walls date from his time. He is said to have imported some two hundred stonemasons from India to build the fort, since masonry was little understood at that time in Kashmir. The works also apparently provided a kind of unemployment relief, since 'A great many persons also got their livelihood from the building of the fort. By means of the pay for their labour, they were brought out from the straits of want.'

The present fort, of eighteenth-century construction, contains a complex of galleries from which there are superb views over the surrounding countryside. A small temple, a courtyard, and the remains of what would appear to be a water garden may also be seen, and in the spring the roofs are carpeted in irises.

The hill of Hari Parbat is linked by a canal to Lake Dal, the head of the canal being marked by a chenar tree of immense dimensions, one of the largest in Kashmir. On the west bank of the lake lies Akbar's other legacy to Srinagar, the garden of Nasim Bagh. Fortress and garden-palace were thus linked in a very practical way: it is still said locally that when times were peaceful Akbar and his followers liked to live at Nasim, but when danger threatened they were able to move up rapidly to the fort.

Nasim Bagh, the Garden of the Breezes, with its eastern aspect and broad shallow terraces rising from the lake, must always have been a place of coolness and refreshment. From here too, the early snows on the mountains opposite are visible. Little remains today of the original work, except for some terrace walls and the ruins of some small buildings near the lake.

The lake-side palace described in Jahangir's memoirs may well have been Nasim Bagh.

'. . . The lake is close to the fort, and the palace overlooks the water. In the palace there was a little garden, with a small building in it in which my revered father used constantly to sit. At this period it

Houseboats at Srinagar. Many, like this one, carry gardens.

Plan of Nasim Bagh.

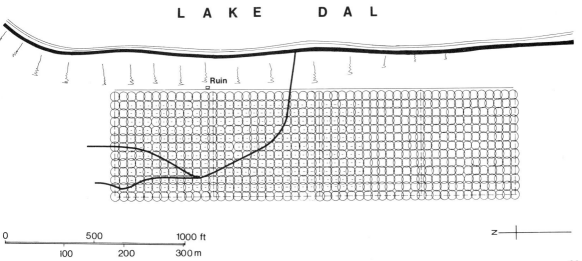

L A K E   D A L

Ruin

0	500	1000 ft
100	200	300 m

Nasim Bagh, Lake Dal, Kashmir. The great block of chenars *planted in Shah Jahan's time stands out clearly across the lake. For centuries* chenars *could be felled only with royal permission.*

Opposite: *Akbar's tomb. A sketch by Peter Mundy of the East India Company, dated about 1632, indicates the richness of the original planting. Some of the architectural features differ from the present garden and there is no trace of the diagonals running inwards from the corners of the enclosing wall, but it seems probable that Mundy only had a glimpse of the tomb, which was sacred and not usually seen by Europeans.*

appeared to me to be very much out of order and ruinous . . . its neglected state did not appear right to me. I ordered Mu'tamid K., who is a servant who knows my temperament, to make every effort to put the little garden in order and repair the buildings. In a short space of time, through his great assiduity, it acquired new beauty. In the garden he put up a lofty terrace 32 yards square, in three divisions, and having repaired the building he adorned it with pictures by master hands and so made it the envy of the picture gallery of China. I call this garden Nur-afza [Light-increasing].

'This year in the little garden of the palace and on the roof of the chief mosque, the tulips blossomed luxuriantly.'

Later, in Shah Jahan's time the site of the garden was planted out with hundreds of chenar trees, on a regular grid. Bisected by a modern road, and with various buildings scattered through it, it is hard to read the overall plan. But seen from a boat, well over into the lake, Nasim Bagh is deeply impressive. The great block of trees, four square almost as if hewn from masonry, is duplicated in the still water of the lake, an immobile piece of geometry set in a matrix of ever-changing clouds and water.

Nasim, earliest of the Mughul gardens in Kashmir, was a place for living in, and as the country took hold upon the imagination and affections of succeeding generations, Nasim was followed by a series of gardens which were primarily summer homes. It is in this that they differ so profoundly from the gardens of the Indian plains which were, in the main, settings for stupendous buildings.

AKBAR'S TOMB, SIKANDRA, NEAR AGRA

The greatest of the Mughuls is buried at Sikandra, that immense pile of building, storey piled on storey, a maze of turrets and staircases leading to white cupolas with views of the limitless plains beyond, the whole set upon a base plan of classical simplicity.

A walled enclosure, something over two thousand feet in each direction, is divided symmetrically by the mausoleum at the centre, into the four-fold plot of Babur's Bagh-i-wafa, the Garden of Fidelity. The tomb stands on a raised platform from which four wide causeways, raised above the surrounding ground level, lead to four gateways. Three of these are stage set-pieces, for entrance is by the south gate, but the pattern of the walks is virtually identical. Four tanks set in the centre platform supplied water to the narrow runnels down the causeways, while a second tank breaks the perspective in each causeway.

The plan is exact, geometrical; dimension repeats dimension, and the whole is finely proportioned to set off the great tomb within it. This is a garden which needs its trees: cypress, pine, plane and palm, for the buildings would be oppressive without them especially now that the irrigation is lacking.

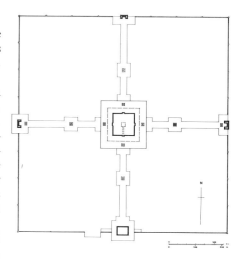

Akbar's tomb at Sikandra, near Agra: plan. The entrance to the tomb, which is below ground level, is shown dotted.

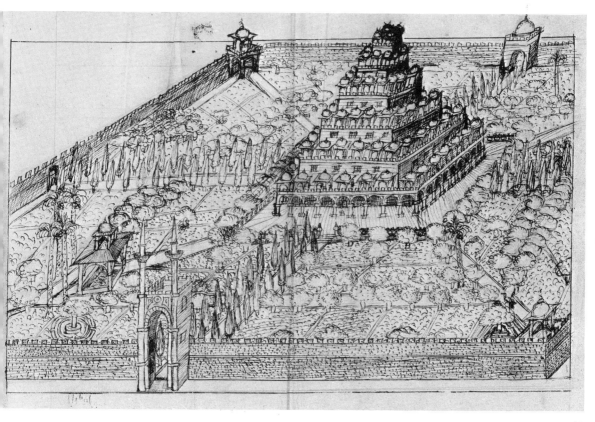

Top: *Akbar's tomb. The entrance gateway seen from the tomb: the cupolas destroyed by the Jats have been restored. Built into the outer edge of the causeway at regular intervals are projecting red sandstone rings, big enough to hold stout poles, with sockets at ground level. This suggests that awnings may have been erected over the causeway.*

Above: *Akbar's tomb. The cross axis, ending in a false gateway. The pattern of round lozenges on the edge of the stone surround to the water-tank in the foreground is one frequently used in Mughul gardens.*

Left: *Akbar's tomb: a photograph taken in the early 1900s. The four lower storeys are of red sandstone, with white marble inlays. The top storey is of white marble. 'That would be approved which the wayfarers of the world should point to as one the like of which was not in the inhabited world' was Jahangir's description of what he thought the tomb should look like.*

The marble cloister surrounding the cenotaph.

The mausoleum was begun in Akbar's lifetime and completed after his death by his son Jahangir. Relations between father and son were often strained and difficult, since Jahangir was a man of violent temper, much given to both drink and opium, while Akbar's long reign had left him impatient to enter his heritage. Jahangir himself refers in his memoirs to the building of Sikandra, and describes how, after his father's death, and while his own attention was diverted by 'the affair of the ill-starred Khusrau' (Jahangir's son, Prince Khusrau, who rebelled and was later put to death) the architects went their own way, and upon his return much of their work had to be dismantled and begun anew.

When the building was complete, Jahangir returned to demonstrate his filial piety, and to observe the necessary ceremonial connected with it.

'On Thursday, the 1st. of the Divine month of Aban, I went on a pilgrimage to the mausoleum of the late King (may the lights of Allah be his testimony) and rubbed the head of supplication on the threshold, the abode of angels . . . All the Begams and other ladies, having sought the blessing of circulating round that shrine, which is the circling place of angels, presented offerings.

On the eve of Friday, a lofty assembly was held of the holy men, the turbaned people [ecclesiastics, etc.] Huffaz [those who recite the Qoran], and singing people, assembled in numbers and practised ecstasies and religious dancing. . . .

The buildings of this blessed mausoleum have been made very lofty.'

Akbar's cenotaph is placed upon the topmost storey, exactly above the actual tomb.

JAHANGIR 1605-1627

The Emperor Jahangir is the central figure in the garden art of
Kashmir. He was the eldest of Akbar's three sons, the princes Salim,
Murad and Daniyal, who were half-brothers. History paints an unattractive picture of them charged with drunkenness, cruelty and
guile, and they appear to have spent much of their time plotting to
supplant one another, and even on occasion their father.

Babur had inherited at the age of eleven, Akbar at thirteen, but
Prince Salim was thirty-six before his accession as emperor. His
father distrusted him and as a result kept him closely in attendance.
Akbar's lively curiosity led him into the most remote corners of his
possessions and there, willingly or unwillingly, for much of the time
Prince Salim had to follow. So, over a long period of time, father and
son came to share in many enterprises.

Jahangir's memoirs are perhaps interesting above all for their
continuity. They trace his developing skill, not only as a garden-
maker, but also as a plantsman and in the understanding of nature
as a whole. Covering some eighteen years, they show him first as a
prince, accompanying his father to Kashmir: visiting the saffron
fields, filled with wonder that the flowers should come before the
leaves. The autumn exceeds his expectations; he hopes one day to
see the spring. . . . So began what was to be a life-long attachment:
'Jehan-Guire became so amorous thereof, that he could not leave it;
and often said, he would rather lose all his Empire, than Kachemire.'

First under Akbar's tutelage, then in his own right as emperor, we
follow the evolution of the gardens. Finally his own son, Khurram,
later the Emperor Shah Jahan, joins him in the finest and most
mature of his achievements, the Shalamar Bagh in Kashmir.

Here was the other side of Jahangir's strange dual nature: his love
of Kashmir, his talent for the potential of a site, and a passion for
plants and flowers which recalled Babur's. All these were to find
expression through the strongest emotion of all, his love for the
woman he married comparatively late in life, the Persian Nur Jahan.

She began life as Mihr-un-Nisa, born in Kandahar of exiled parents.
A popular legend tells how she was already promised to another
when the young Prince Salim's choice fell upon her. Akbar refused
to allow his son to intervene, and she was duly married and became
the mother of a daughter. So far the tale is almost certainly fictional.
It seems clear, however, that at some point, her husband, Sher
Afgan, for quite other reasons, became inconvenient to Jahangir.

*Portrait of Jahangir (the 'World-seizer'),
painted by Abu-' l-Hasan. The emperor is
standing on a globe (of European type), fixed
in a stand. Beneath the globe is an ox and
beneath the ox a large fish (it was a popular
Islamic notion that the earth was supported
by a great fish). The chain suspended from the
javelin probably represented the chain of
justice which Jahangir had hung from the
battlements of Agra fort, so that the oppressed
might attract his attention.*

A pretext was found for his murder and his widow was brought, a virtual prisoner, to the court. Here she lived for the next few years upon a tiny pittance. Then, possibly through the intervention of her brother, Asaf Khan, the emperor determined upon marriage with her. A remarkable aspect of the whole affair was that by this time she must have been about thirty-four, an age at which women in India were already considered old.

The marriage took place in splendour and for the rest of their lives together he remained devoted to her. 'Before I married her I never knew what marriage was,' writes Jahangir, and the honours which he paid her were unprecedented. She received the titles first of Nur Mahal (the Light of the Palace) and then of Nur Jahan (the Light of the World), and shared every attribute of royalty apart from the prayer for the sovereign.

A woman of great distinction and many interests, she was a talented designer, whether of gardens, golden ornaments, or palace interiors; she arranged great feasts, wrote poems in Persian. On another level, she cared for the poor and the dispossessed, and made the cause of orphan girls especially her own.

There seems to be little doubt that she was the directing force behind the prodigious output of every kind, palaces, pavilions, tombs and gardens, on which they embarked together. They visited Kashmir many times, variously described as from six to thirteen. The visits were long ones, sometimes the whole summer, and the gardens, some of them begun when he was still a prince, were progressively extended and improved. The royal gardens, Shalamar, Achabal and Vernag, belong to this period, together with Nur Jahan's own garden, known as Jarogha Bagh on Lake Manasbal. Meanwhile her brother, Asaf Khan, was developing Nishat Bagh, the largest and most spectacular of all.

Jahangir's memoirs describe in detail the flowers and the feasting, the minutiae of measurements, the depths of water, the dimensions of a canal. Yet a gap remains; he writes little that is personal, and one would like to know more of their way of life in the splendid summer homes that they created. Nor did he neglect the rest of Kashmir. He had the length and breadth of the country measured, visited the upland margs, or meadows, where as many as fifty different kinds of wild flowers were recorded, and made a grand procession by boat to see the illuminations for the river festival in Srinagar.

The usual routes into Kashmir were by Bhimbar and the Pir Panjal passes; or by the Kishan Ganga and Baramula, open a little earlier in the year. Neither could have been easy, and Jahangir gave instructions for the building of a number of *sarais*, or resthouses along the way 'for the accommodation of myself and the ladies, for in the cold weather one should not be in tents'.

He took with him at times some unexpected travelling companions, for he had his father's easy tolerance of alien races and religions. The Italian Jesuit missionary, for instance, Father de Castro, complains feelingly of the terrors and privations of the journey, whereas the emperor writes of the beauties of nature which he enjoyed on the way. Waterfalls especially pleased him immensely. One he watched by the hour and at another, at Bahramgalla, he ordered a terrace to be put up, so that all his courtiers might admire the view.

A perhaps more important visitor was Sir Thomas Roe. Appointed ambassador to the 'Great Mogul' by James I, he spent some four years promoting the cause of British trade in India. The emperor received him in great state and took him travelling in his company. Roe has left a lively account of his adventures, including a description of the five hundred elephants of the procession, and the loss of one of his own baggage ponies to a lion.

Kashmir was Jahangir's first love always, but little of the empire remained unvisited. He travelled to Kabul, to see Babur's gardens there, and saw no less than seven in one day. It was a happy, if exhausting, occasion, for he competed with his courtiers in leaping streams, and by the end of the day confessed that he had never walked so far in his life. Evidently attracted, he bought land there soon afterwards, and laid out a garden himself, which he called the 'World-Adorning'.

Elaborate arrangements for travel, together with direct personal rule, meant that the Mughul court and capital tended to be wherever, for the time being, it suited the emperor. Delhi was not yet the splendid city it became under Shah Jahan, and Jahangir divided his time, when in India, between Agra, Ajmer and Lahore.

In Agra, Babur's gardens had been maintained in good condition, while Nur Jahan had appropriated the Nur-Afshan garden for her own use. Here she celebrated the sixteenth year of her husband's reign. At Ajmer, successive rulers had added their contribution. Humayun restored the Dargah shrine, one of the holiest places of the empire, while Akbar built a mosque. A place of pilgrimage for Muslims, Akbar visited Ajmer so regularly from Agra and Fatehpur Sikri that he set up *kos minars*, great columns corresponding to milestones, along the way. Here Jahangir frequently held court, and it was here, in 1616, that he first received Sir Thomas Roe.

But it was perhaps Lahore which became, in a special sense, Jahangir's capital since, much further north than Delhi, it shortened the journey to Kashmir. Parts of Lahore fort are attributed to him, including the so-called Quadrangle of Jahangir. Outside the city lay the woodlands where he loved to hunt. He could be sentimental as well as cruel, and near his hunting-lodge, he built a tower and drinking-pool for animals, in memory of a pet deer.

By contrast, at Ahmadabad, in the twelfth year of his reign, he wrote:

'At this time the gardener represented that a servant of Muqarrab Khan had cut down some *champa* trees above the bench alongside the river. On hearing this I became angry, and went myself to enquire into the matter and to exact satisfaction. When it was established that this improper act had been committed by him, I ordered both his thumbs to be cut off as a warning to others.'

Near Lahore, too, Nur Jahan laid out yet another immense garden, the Dilkusha at Shahdara. Here at the last they were buried; Jahangir in a tomb of his wife's designing in the gardens themselves, Nur Jahan and her brother not far away.

Beautiful and distinguished, Nur Jahan has perhaps been over-romanticized as Jahangir's beloved empress. Her ability, strength of character and driving ambition made her the virtual ruler of India. More and more, power came to be concentrated in her hands. Jahangir wrote 'I have conferred the duties of government upon her, I shall be satisfied if I have a *ser* of wine and half a *ser* of meat per diem.' He was content to have it so; to indulge his weaknesses and enjoy his pleasures, while Nur Jahan relieved him of the tedium of statesmanship, her father and brother always at her side. If, little by little, there was a departure from Akbar's high standards, the empire remained cohesive, and was to so do for more than a hundred years.

Yet such was the mystique vested in the person of the emperor, that with his death her influence vanished utterly. She and Jahangir had had no children, but Jahangir's younger son, Shahriyar, had married the daughter of her own first marriage to Sher Afgan. Nur Jahan made a brief attempt to place him on the throne, but he was killed, most likely at the instigation of Asaf Khan, who declared his loyalty to the rightful heir. Nur Jahan herself lived on, in retirement and obscurity, until the age of seventy-two, a pensioner of Shah Jahan.

SHALAMAR BAGH, KASHMIR

'In these two or three days I frequently embarked in a boat and was delighted to go round and look at the flowers of Phak and Shalamar . . . Shalamar is near the lake. It has a pleasant stream which comes down from the hills and flows into the Dal Lake. I bade my son Khurram [Shah Jahan] dam it up and make a waterfall, which it would be a pleasure to behold. This place is one of the sights of Kashmir.'

Memoirs of Jahangir, 1620

'The most admirable of all these Gardens is that of the King, which is called Chahlimar. From the Lake, one enters into it by a great Canal, border'd with great green Turfs. This Canal is above five hundred common paces long, and runs 'twixt two large Allees of Poplars: It leadeth to a great Cabinet in the midst of the Garden, where begins another Canal far more magnificent, which runs with a little rising unto the end of the Garden. This Canal is paved with large Free-Stone; its sloping side cover'd with the same; and in the midst of it, there is a long Row of Jets of Water, from 15 to 15 foot. There are also from space to space, great Rounds of Water serving for Storehouses, whence many Jets of Water, variously figured, do spring up: And this Canal ends at another great Cabinet, which is almost like the first.

These Cabinets, which are in a manner made like Domes, situate in the middle of the Canal, and encompassed with Water, and consequently between those two great Allees of Poplars, have a Gallery that reigneth round about, and four Gates opposite to one another; two of which do respect the Allees, with two Bridges to pass over, one on one side, and the other on the other; the other two look upon the opposite Canals. Each Cabinet consists of a great Chamber in the midst of four other lesser Chambers, which are in the four Corners: All is painted and guilded within, the great Chamber as well as the little ones, having Sentences with great Letters, in the Persian Tongue written upon them. The four Gates are very rich;

they are made of great Stones with two Columns, taken from those ancient Idol-Temples, ruin'd by Chah-Jahan. The price of these great Stones and Pillars is not well known, nor what kind of Stone they be; though it appears sufficiently, that 'tis a sort of precious Stone finer than Marble or Porphyre.'

Francois Bernier, 1665

Shalamar Bagh, Kashmir. The approach along the canal from Lake Dal.

Shalamar, most celebrated of the Lake Dal gardens, is also the most secluded. The journey across the lake is slow, the boat pushing its way through the tightly packed lotus, and there is time — time to watch the brilliant kingfishers, to enjoy the reflections in the lake and to speculate where Shalamar may lie among the trees on the far shore. Presently, one enters a canal, flanked on either side by trees, with occasional views of the fields beyond, or the timber houses on the bank. The perspective narrows, the journey becomes yet slower, the boat slides imperceptibly to a halt by the roots of a great tree and at the head of the canal lies one of the loveliest gardens of the world.

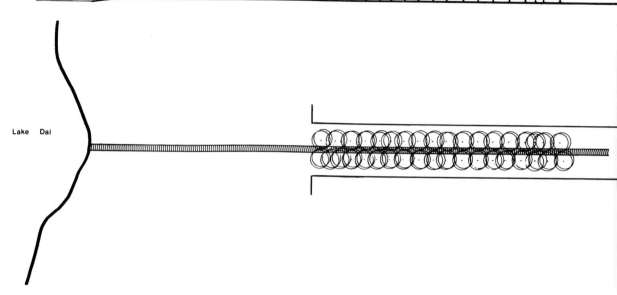

The emperor's throne seen from within the Diwan-i-Am. Today the water only flows in spring, when the snows are melting and the streams are swollen.

Lake   Dal

First laid out by Jahangir, and surely much influenced by Nur Jahan, Shalamar combines a refinement of detail and proportion with an all-pervading peace and calm, which yet escapes melancholy. Here is the 'paradise within a paradise'. The lake, so recently crossed, is now invisible, yet very much present in the mind. The mountains lie behind, yet they do not tower and dominate as at Nishat Bagh or Chasma Shahi. The encirclement is gentle, the mountains glimpsed only occasionally between breaks in the trees. Even the little world of road and river, seen only from the upper storey of a gazebo, is itself a secret, enclosed one, far removed from the busy ricefields and distant snows which enliven the view from Achabal.

The design is simple. At the head of the garden, the small river from the fields is diverted into a broad shallow canal leading to the wide rectangular basin in which the main black marble pavilion is set, surrounded on all sides by fountains and water. Changes of level are in general slight, and must have been to a great extent deliberately contrived to give a sense of containment and repose. Canal, building and plane trees are splendidly related to one another in scale, and in autumn, when the trees turn scarlet, in colour also.

It is this great pavilion in the zenana garden that provides the climax at Shalamar and seems, like a magnet, to draw the whole of the garden to its heart – the central point from which four vistas open. The impact is through breadth and simplicity, together with an

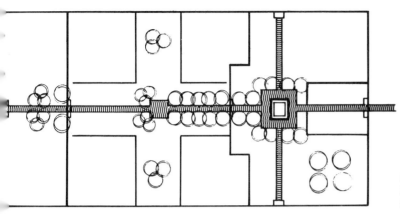

Shalamar Bagh, Kashmir.
Plan showing the garden and approach canal
in relation to the lake.

The Diwan-i-Am, or Hall of Public Audience,
from a water-colour by Constance Villiers
Stuart. The emperor sat on his black marble
throne above the water.

Shalamar Bagh, Kashmir.
The water throne in the garden of the
Diwan-i-Khas, or Hall of Private Audience.
The Diwan itself was almost certainly built
across the central cascade. The constantly
recurring decoration of round lozenges on the
stonework quite possibly derives from the log
ends of earlier wooden constructions.

unerring sense of proportion, rather than from any high drama or *tour-de-force* of construction.

Below, the design broadens, opens more to the sunlight, becomes a little more sophisticated, the changes in level a little sharper, till it finally reaches the Diwan-i-Am, the Hall of Public Audience, where the emperor sat on his black marble throne above the water, which was led through the building to fall in a small cascade into the lowest pool. Originally, this part of the garden led directly to the canal, and the visual scale must have been greatly extended. As in many of the other gardens, the approach today has been truncated by a modern road.

It may not be too fanciful here to draw in one respect a parallel with Venice. At whatever cost in time, the first approach to each should be by water, since both are works of art born of water and both in recollection are inseparable from the wide translucent waters around them.

Historically, the garden is the work of both Jahangir and Shah Jahan. The choice of site was Jahangir's, and Shah Jahan joined him in the design when he was still a prince. It was then known as Farah-Baksh, the Bestower of Joy, for the name Shalamar is of far older provenance. It is said to date from the reign of Pravarasena II, who built a house here in the sixth century AD, calling it Shalamar, the Abode of Love.

The black marble pavilion, built by Shah Jahan. The original jets would have sent up solid plumes of water rather than sprays.

The black pavilion in late summer, showing the depth of the surrounding tank. Arcades under the causeway allow the free movement of water.

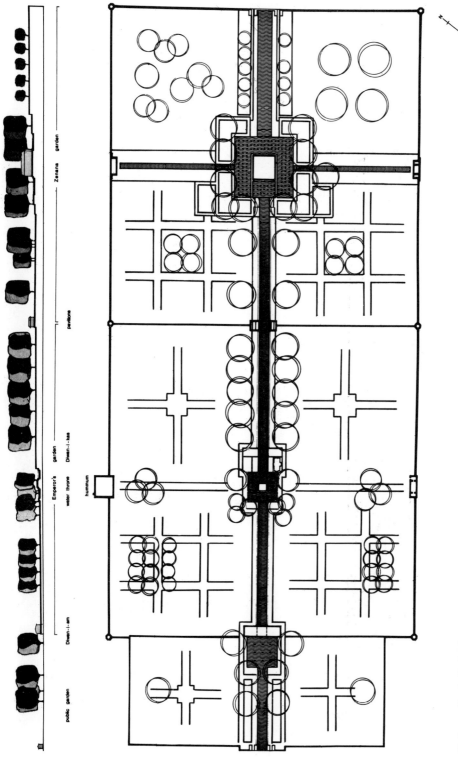

Shalamar Bagh, Kashmir.
Plan and section of the garden.

Above: *Looking back from the black pavilion at the canal which so impressed Bernier. But the water is only a few inches deep.*

The cascade above the black pavilion. A sharp drop in levels was necessary at this point to provide sufficient head of water to force the water through the large number of jets in the tank round the pavilion. Below the two ledges over which the water flows into the tank are double rows of chini-kanas, or pigeon holes, in which lights were placed behind the sheets of falling water.

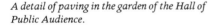
Water from the tank round the black pavilion not only falls over a central cascade, but is also passed through slits at the sides to create further expanses of shallow water before being returned to the central canal.

After his accession, Shah Jahan extended the design to the north and built the black marble pavilion in the zenana garden. The work was carried out in 1630 by Zafar Khan, the Mughul Governor of Kashmir, and the new part of the garden was named the Faiz-Baksh, the Bestower of Bounties. The pavilion with its open sides is possibly the finest authentic example of a Mughul *baradari*, although it has been much altered. In particular, the dome mentioned by Bernier has been replaced by a three-tiered roof and the doors have disappeared; the painted decoration also is mid-nineteenth century. The *baradaris* of the Ana Sagar garden at Ajmer, built by Shah Jahan, deserve comparison. Other changes too have come about. There is no trace of the 'rounds of water' (circular basins) of Bernier's day, neither is there the same profusion of fruit as in Mughul times. Once the garden was full of grapes, apples, almonds and peaches. The vines may well have been trained on pergolas, for Baron Huegel mentions such a feature in 1835, although the date of its construction is uncertain. Another lower garden, with connecting water-channels, was also apparently laid out by Shah Jahan, but no trace of it remains.

Less showy than Nishat Bagh, less worldly than Achabal, the sheer quality of Shalamar reminds us that here two emperors contributed their finest gifts: Jahangir his flair for site, and Shah Jahan his capacity for magnificence in building. The same Persian quotation appears at Shalamar as at the Red Fort in Delhi: 'If there be a Paradise on the face of the earth, it is here, it is here, it is here!'

ACHABAL, KASHMIR

'From this stage [Kanabal] H.M. went off on the horse of fortune to see the fountain of Alanj [Achabal] which is a delightful place for visitors, and a place of worship of the ancients. There is a limpid reservoir and the water always shoots up [from the earth]. Occasionally a beautiful yellow spotted fish appears, and whenever this occurs, the year is reckoned a fortunate one. It appeared about this time, and caused great joy.'

The Akbar-nama, 1589

A detail of paving in the garden of the Hall of Public Audience.

'On Tuesday the 31st. pitched at the fountain of Achval. The water of this spring is more plentiful than that of the other [Vernag] and it has a fine water fall. Around it lofty plane-trees and graceful white poplars, bringing their heads together, have made enchanting places to sit in.

'As far as one could see, in a beautiful garden, *Ja'fari* [*Tagetes patula*] flowers had bloomed, so that one might say it was a piece of Paradise.'

Memoirs of Jahangir, 1620

'Returning from Send-Brary I turn'd a little aside from the road to go and lye at Achiavel, which is a House of pleasure of the ancient Kings of Kachemire, and at present of the Great Mogol. That which most adorns it is a Fountain, the water whereof diffuseth it self on all sides round about that Fabrick (which is not despicable) and into the Gardens by an hundred Canals. It breaks out of the Earth, as if by some violence it ascended up from the bottom of a Well, and that

Achabal.
A branch of a chenar *sweeps down beside the great cascade.*

103

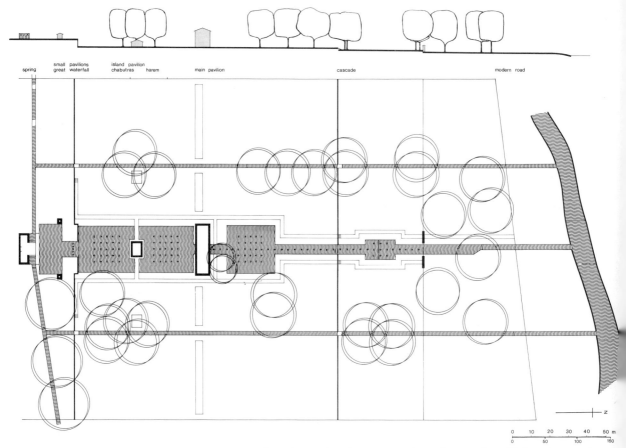

spring | small pavilions | island pavilion | main pavilion | cascade | modern road
great waterfall | chabutras harem

0 10 20 30 40 50 m
0 50 100 150

Achabal, near Islamabad, Kashmir. Plan and section.

The side chadars *at Achabal roar and foam, very different from the silent ripples of Nishat or Chasma Shahi.*

Opposite, below : *The water gushes out from the spring in a white plume across the reservoir above the cascade, to build up the pressure for the necessary head of water for the whole garden.* Above : *The lowest terrace.*

with such an abundance as might make it to be called a River rather than a Fountain. The water of it is admirably good, and so cold that one can hardly endure to hold ones hand in it. The Garden it self is very fine, there being curious Walks in it, and store of Fruit-bearing Trees, of Apples, Pears, Prunes, Apricocks and Cherries, and many jets of waters of various figures, and Ponds replenish'd with Fish, together with a very high Cascata of water, which by its fall maketh a great Nape of thirty or forty paces long, which hath an admirable effect, especially in the night, when under this Nape there is put a great number of little Lamps fitted in holes purposely made in the Wall; which maketh a curious shew.'

Francois Bernier, 1665

Achabal, like Vernag, lies close by the old direct road to Srinagar, where the Vale of Kashmir runs out abruptly to the south, against the great hills. This was the old Jammu route, which generations of travellers and pilgrims had followed, over the difficult roads and terraced fields.

There were other ways, by Bhimbar and the Pir Panjal passes, which Jahangir crossed with elephants; and the easier, longer route up the Jhelum valley. Yet there could perhaps be no more dramatic introduction to Kashmir than these two sites where the water rises out of the hills with such power.

The spring itself is an ancient and sacred one, its original name being Akshavala, and it had been a place of pilgrimage for centuries. Akbar visited it, and the excellence of the water was remarked on by both Abu-'l-Fazl and Bernier. This was something to which both Mughuls and Kashmiris attached great importance. Jahangir considered the water of the Lar valley to be the best in all Kashmir and paid Haidar Malik thirty thousand rupees to bring down Lar water in a canal to Akbar's garden at Srinagar. By contrast, one reason given for Akbar's early desertion of Fatehpur Sikri was that the water supply there was unsatisfactory.

Most Kashmiri gardens are best seen in spring, since the water is later diverted to feed the ricefields, and the summer visitor can sympathize with Asaf Khan when Shah Jahan cut off the stream from his garden at Nishat Bagh. But at Achabal there is water and to spare. Of all the gardens, it seems the one most committed to the outside world. There is a sense of urgency and abundance in the water: it glitters in the sun: and both in sound and speed of flow excels the other gardens as it hurries away to the villages beyond. From the high terrace, long views open over the fertile countryside to the snow mountains beyond, and here, too, the palms and planes of the valley meet the firs and deodars of the hills.

The spring pours out at the foot of the hill, for as at Vernag, the mountains rise sharply from the plain. Little remains of the pavilion which once housed the spring, and the water spills first into a reservoir and then over the great waterfall which is the climax of the garden. No other site has so splendid a feature, and it is fortunate that the intensity of the flow matches the vigour and imagination of the design.

Achabal.
The main pavilion from the island; all the pavilions are Kashmiri, built on the stone bases of the former Mughul structures.

Opposite: *Looking through the archway of the main pavilion: the smaller pavilion is on an island, reached by raised stone causeways. The foreground fountain jet is more authentic than the sprays.*

107

Achabal.
Beside the canals, solid stone platforms are set
between some of the chenars.

The waterfall is flanked by two small summer-houses, where its thunder can be enjoyed in its fullest intensity. Bernier refers to lamps under the cascade. These were probably the simple clay bowls, with oil and a floating wick, which have been used in India for centuries for illuminations, and the effect, with shimmering water and flickering light, must have been wholly enchanting.

Below lie wide pools enlivened by fountains, a pleasant island pavilion set within them. Below again, the water passes under a larger pavilion, and down the length of the garden to fall with undiminished force over the final change of level. On either side, water rushes down two tall *chadars* or chutes into long canals brimming level with the ground, passing under huge trees, where two stone platforms contrast in their utter stillness with the sound and movement of the water.

Primarily the creation of Nur Jahan, Achabal was at one time called Begamabad after her. What, one wonders, was the character of its Mughul pavilions in her day? In all the gardens there have been considerable changes in the buildings, which today are mostly Kashmiri, of later date and indigenous character. Buildings there certainly were, palaces at Nasim Bagh and Vernag, Bernier's 'Fabrick' set among the waters at Achabal, and later Shah Jahan's splendid zenana pavilion at Shalamar, Dara Shukoh's water palace at Peri Mahal. It is possible, however, that many of the smaller platforms, or *chabutras*, were never originally intended for buildings at all, but simply as bases to take a series of decorative tents and awnings. This had been the case earlier: a painting of Humayun's birth-feast shows just such a platform, spread with a carpet, and over it a decorative canopy. In her *Humayun-nama*, too, Gulbadan Begam describes her arrival in India and an outdoor meal: 'There was a raised platform on a pleasant spot, and a pavilion of red cloth, with a lining of Gujarati brocade, and six canopies of silk and brocade, each of a different colour, and a square enclosure of cloth and painted poles.'

The spatial patterns must have been finer: substantial buildings contrasted with simple platforms, usually over or near running water, where the owner could sit, either on a carpet in the open air or under some light-hearted canopy put up for the occasion. The present scatter of small pavilions, built on the old Mughul foundations, is less satisfactory, although many are charming in themselves. At Achabal, for instance, one would gladly exchange the stiff sentry-boxes each side of the waterfall for some colourful and impermanent awning waving in the breeze.

Today, the fruit trees have largely disappeared and Achabal is a garden of open spaces, people and water. Light and shade have the fullest play, for the cascades are tilted so that they may catch the sun and the fast-moving water sparkles in the canals. Overhead, the light is filtered through the great planes, and only in the pavilions are there occasional deep shadows.

A royal prince entertaining guests (period of Babur). The tent and carpets correspond closely with Gulbadan Begam's descriptions in the Humayun-nama.

From the octagonal pool water flows under the central arch of the ruined palace into a long canal.

Opposite, above: *Vernag. Plan.*

Below: *The great canal. The mountain behind drops sharply down, giving a sidelong view up a gentler valley.*

VERNAG, KASHMIR

'The source of the Bihat is a spring in Kashmir called the Vir-nag; in the language of India a snake is *vir-nag*. Clearly there had been a large snake at that place.

I went twice to the spring in my father's lifetime. . . . It is an octagonal reservoir about twenty yards by twenty. . . . The water is exceedingly pure. Although I could not guess its depth, a grain of poppy seed is visible until it touches the bottom. There were many fish to be seen in it.

After my accession, I ordered them to build the sides of the spring round with stone, and they made a garden round it with a canal; and built halls and houses about it, and made a place such that travellers over the world can point out few like it.'

'On Wednesday, the 1st. of Mihr, marching from Achval, I pitched camp near the fountain of Virnag. . . .

When I was a prince, I had given an order that they should erect a building at this spring suitable to the place. It was now completed. . . . Of the trimness of the canal and the verdure of the grass that grew below the fountain, what can one write? Various sorts of plants and sweet-smelling herbs grew there in profusion, and among them was seen a stem [*buta*], which had exactly the appearance of the variegated tail of a peacock. It waved about in the ripple, and bore flowers here and there.

In short, in the whole of Kashmir there is no sight of such beauty and enchanting character.

It appears to me that what is upstream in Kashmir bears no comparison with what is downstream. One should stay some days in these regions and go round them so as to enjoy oneself thoroughly.

As the hour for marching was near, and snow was beginning to fall at the head of the passes, I had not the leisure to linger there, and was obliged to turn my rein towards the city.

I gave an order that plane trees should be planted on both sides, of the banks of the canal above mentioned.'

Memoirs of Jahangir, 1620

'From Achiavel I went yet a little more out of my way to pass through another Royal Garden, which is also very beautiful, and hath the same pleasantness with that of Achiavel, but this is peculiar in it, that in one of its Ponds there are Fishes that come when they are called, and when you cast bread to them; the biggest whereof have golden rings in their Noses, with inscriptions about them, which they say that renowned Nour-Mehalle, the Wife of Jehan-Guire, the Grandfather of Aureng-Zebe, caused to be fastened in them.'

Francois Bernier, 1665

Jahangir and Nur Jahan reputedly loved Vernag above all other places. It is not hard to understand their reasons. It has a remoteness which makes the very act of arrival something to be treasured. Akbar himself had encountered difficulties. After visiting Achabal, he went on to hunt, and 'his idea was that he would proceed on to the fountain here of the Bihat (Vernag), but rain and the slipperiness of the defiles restrained him from this plan'.

Like Achabal, the spring at Vernag had long been a place of worship. In this case, the name derives from snake-worship, an ancient religion of Kashmir, of which Abu-'l-Fazl instances seven hundred shrines. The spring comes up in a deep pool, at the foot of

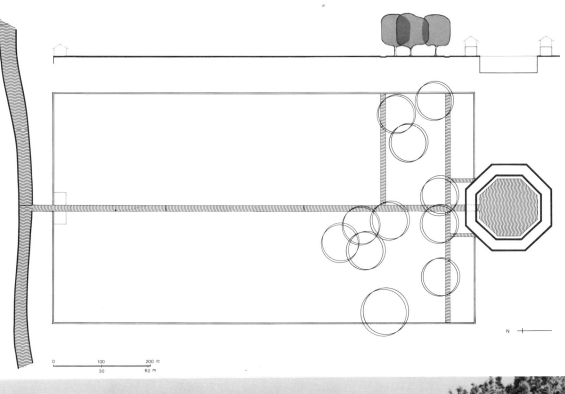

the hills below the Banihal pass, and is usually considered to be the source of the Jhelum river.

Jahangir's memoirs describe the buildings round the pool, and two inscriptions testify to the builders: 'The King raised this building to the skies: the angel Gabriel suggested its date – 1609.' and 'God be praised! what a canal and what a waterfall! constructed by Haidar, by order of the King of the World, the Paramount Lord of his Age, this canal is a type of the canal in Paradise, this waterfall is the glory of Kashmir.'

The spring is enclosed in an octagonal tank, with arcaded recesses all round. The arches appear a little stunted, and this may well be due to a later raising of levels for irrigation. Little remains, however, of the original buildings both north and south of the reservoir. To the north, the water is released to fill the main canal, some twelve feet wide and nearly a thousand feet long to the point where it discharges to feed the river. A second, smaller canal forms a cross axis and there are traces of other buildings, attributed to Shah Jahan.

Yet to describe the buildings is to convey nothing of the special quality of Vernag. Landscape and geometry combine to make an unforgettable whole. Since much of the palace has disappeared, the remaining design is of the simplest; an octagon and a long canal. Its quality lies in the upward thrust of the background hills, clothed with deodars; in the arcaded court below them, surrounding the spring, blue-green and full of great fish as in Jahangir's day; in the immense length of the central channel, dominating the big level garden and imposing a symmetry which at the last is suddenly broken by a diagonal view up the adjoining valley.

One remembers Vernag for these two surprises: at one end the casual entrance through the low arch, dark, unimportant, and then the sunlit tank with its complex of domes and niches, its colour and its stillness; at the bottom of the garden, the slanted glimpse up the hitherto unseen valley draws down the skyline, breaking what might otherwise be overpowering enclosure and bringing a gentler counterpoint of poplar and meadow to the mountain background.

Here Jahangir had wished to be buried. Travelling for the last time, he died near Rajauri, asking that his body should be brought down and buried beside the spring at Vernag. Once again the difficulties of the journey proved intimidating, and instead, the *cortège* returned bringing the emperor back for burial at Lahore.

A drawing of Vernag by Captain Knight, published in 1863, shows the buildings then existing over the entrance to the octagonal tank. They are probably Kashmiri, on the original Mughul foundations.

Miniature of Asaf Khan IV.

NISHAT BAGH, KASHMIR

Nishat Bagh, the Garden of Gladness, one of the non-royal gardens on Lake Dal, is also the largest and most spectacular. Its attribution is something of a puzzle, since it is generally credited to 'Asaf Khan'. The probable owner was Abu-'l-Hasan, the elder brother of Nur Jahan, to whom Jahangir had given the title of Asaf Khan IV, a kind of Grand Vizier. Alternatively, he may have been the previous holder of the title, Asaf Khan III, a former governor of Kashmir and a great horticulturist.

It is, however, tempting to suppose him to have been Nur Jahan's brother, and to imagine a collaboration between herself, her brother and the emperor. Yet Nishat Bagh lacks the refinement and sureness of touch which we associate with Nur Jahan. It is on a monumental scale, a set piece designed to be seen from water level and mounting in an almost overwhelming progression of terraces to the final dramatic backcloth of the mountains behind.

Nishat Bagh, Lake Dal. To get to Nishat by
water one passes under a bridge set in the bund.

It is a place to be approached by boat, sliding under a steeply angled bridge into a hitherto unsuspected inner lake. On the far shore, a pavilion is reflected, a mirror image in the water, and above it a stupendous garden. There were once twelve changes of level, one for each sign of the Zodiac, but the same modern road that truncates Shalamar cuts off the bottom terraces from the garden. From the lake it is seen as it always was, the firm base of the lowest walls underlying and underpinning the whole design and reaching out to the two clumps of trees at water level, which contain the composition as surely as a frame.

The colour is astonishing: brown walls, brown tree trunks, great trees which change throughout the seasons, solid against the shadowy blues and greys of the mountain above. The pavilion, with its echoing pink triangles of roof, has a certain sugar-plum charm from the lake. From within the garden, however, its siting is unhappy. For here is probably the finest outward view of them all; less romantic than that from Chasma Shahi, it has the pureness and inevitability of a drawing in wash. The lake has a quality of translucence; the bridge and bund are sharp, yet somehow unreal, with Hari Parbat and the distant snow mountains in receding planes behind. Into this, clumsily, at every level, intrudes the pavilion. Once the ground floor contained fountains, and was open back and front, so that the water design flowed almost uninterrupted to the

The approach to the gardens across the inner lake. The effect of the lower terraces can still be seen, reaching out to the two clumps of chenars which frame the whole design and relate it to the grand scale of the mountains behind.

On either side of the central axis, with its canal flanked by smooth lawns and flower beds, is the traditional orchard.

Nishat Bagh.
Looking down towards the lake.

From the upper floor of the pavilion.

lake. Now, with the openings walled up, it presents a solid obstacle, blocking the very prospect that would lift the garden into greatness. Only when the topmost, zenana, terrace is reached does the whole lovely scene come into view unhindered. Since Nishat Bagh was not a royal garden, with all the need for protocol and ceremonial that this involved, there are two divisions only, the pleasure garden and the zenana terrace. The main feature is the great central watercourse, some thirteen feet wide. It is treated as a series of canals, each dropping by a cascade to the terrace below. The canals are full of fountain jets, and each change of level is modelled and accentuated: by flights of steps, by reflecting pools, or – a special feature of Nishat Bagh – by a number of stone and marble thrones placed across the water. These thrones are the perfect complement to the canals; they do not block the view, yet to sit upon them, with the water rushing underneath, cooling the air, must have been a delight. The whole design is flanked by avenues of very tall chenars, and the garden is seen at its flamboyant best in the autumn, the red and gold of the trees set off by the blue mountains behind.

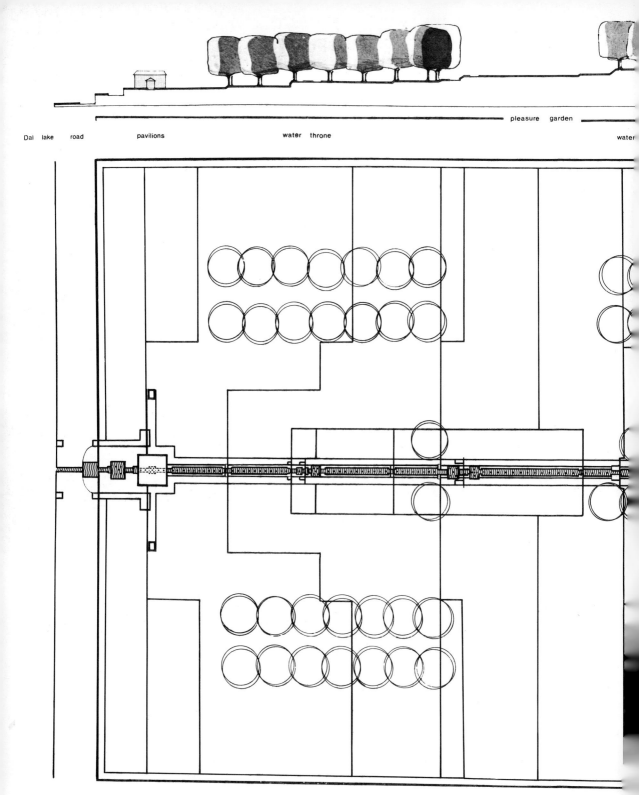

pleasure garden

Dal lake   road   pavilions   water throne   water

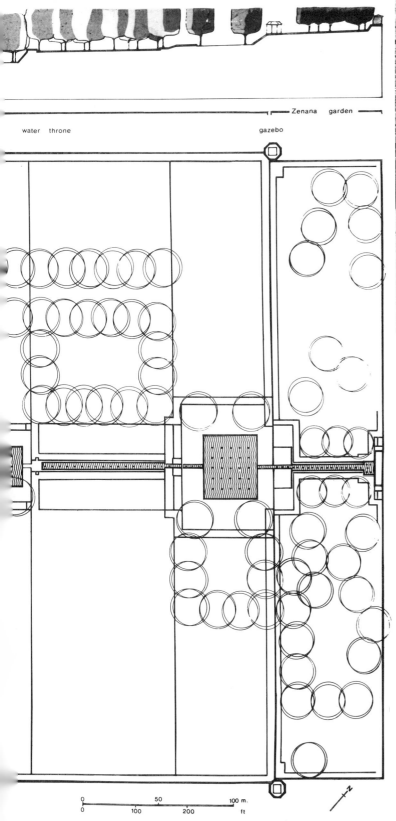

water throne

Zenana garden

gazebo

0 50 100 m.
0 100 200 ft

Top: *A stone seat set above a rippling* chadar. *The planting is of cockscomb, beloved by both the Mughuls and the Kashmiris.*

A detail shows the construction allowing water to flow beneath a stone seat.

Nishat Bagh. Plan and section.

119

Nishat Bagh.
One of the corner pavilions looking out upon the world.

Detail of chadar *patterns.*

The retaining wall of the zenana terrace, nearly twenty feet high and running the full width of the garden, is one of its finest features. The wall is faced with a series of repeating arches, with a suggestion of linked pilasters between them. Warm, honey-coloured, patterned with sun and shadow, it is perfectly in scale with the big chenars. The gazebos at either end are striking. Three storeys in all, with a staircase throughout, the lowest storey echoes the design of the retaining wall. The middle floor, at zenana level, is the principal one, with balconied openings, while from the upper turret sidelong views reveal yet another world. Terraced ricefields give way to poplars, and beyond them is the lake, with glimpses of the life and buildings on its far shore – doubtless all that the ladies of the zenana would ever see.

There is a story told that Shah Jahan, in later years, saw the garden and coveting it, tried to persuade his father-in-law to make it over to him. Asaf Khan refused, for it was his dearest possession. The belief being current amongst the Mughuls that a garden can only be bought for a fair price or given in friendship, as otherwise it will bring bad luck, the emperor was unable to enforce his wish. Infuriated, he ordered the stream above to be diverted, leaving Asaf Khan disconsolate among his silent fountains. A servant, risking his life, restored the flow. The emperor relented, and Nishat was itself again.

Nur Jahan's memorial to her parents stands on the river bank at
Agra, not far from Babur's Ram Bagh. It celebrates a family whose
astonishing rise to fortune reads like fiction. Ghiyas Beg, a Persian
poet, had been forced by circumstance to flee his native Tehran.
With his wife, two sons and a daughter he reached Kandahar a
refugee. They had been robbed on the way and left with only two
mules, which the family took turns to ride. Having arrived in
Kandahar, his wife gave birth to another daughter. This was
Mihr-un-Nisa, who was to become the Empress Nur Jahan.

Ghiyas Beg first took service with Akbar, and later, in Jahangir's
reign, was awarded the title of I'timad-ud-Daula. He survived a

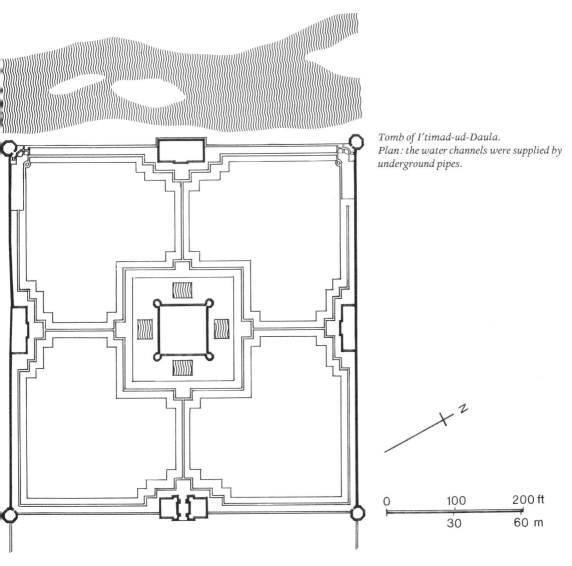

Tomb of I'timad-ud-Daula.
Plan: the water channels were supplied by
underground pipes.

The tomb of I'timad-ud-Daula, Agra.
The front entrance.

The cross axis: the false gateway is of red
sandstone with white inlays.

period of disgrace, when he was suspected of implication in a plot to set Jahangir's eldest son Khusrau on the throne. He was imprisoned, but later set free on payment of a substantial fine. However, following his daughter's marriage to the emperor, he became first treasurer and then prime minister, being allowed the rare privilege of beating his drum at court.

Together with his son and daughter, he formed one of the triumvirate which came to exercise the real power of India. He died in 1622, of a broken heart according to Jahangir, for his wife had died three months earlier. The Imperial couple were recalled from a journey to Kashmir, and arrived just in time to reach his deathbed. Thus both Nur Jahan's parents are commemorated at Agra.

The graceful, intensely feminine design was an innovation in many ways. As might be expected, nature was the dominant theme, and the trees and flowers in the inlays are remarkably life-like. Carried out in *pietra-dura* (an inlay of semi-precious stones into marble) they show one of the earliest uses of this technique, later to be used to great effect in the Taj Mahal. Octagonal towers at the four corners are a particular feature and the whole design is thought to have provided the model for Jahangir's own tomb at Lahore.

The gatehouse is approached by a straight drive, with orchards on either side, regularly planted. They are a reminder of the planting once general in such gardens, when their produce provided funds for the upkeep of the garden after the death of the owner, when the

Top: *The waterfront pavilion from the top of the tomb;* above, *detail of inlay on the water front pavilion.*

123

The tomb of I'timad-ud-Daula.
Interior view by an Agra or Delhi artist, about
1828. Pen and water-colour.

I'timad-ud-Daula.

tomb was left in the care of priests. This probably accounts for the higher survival rate of the tomb-gardens as against the pleasure gardens. Not until the nineteenth century was the restoration of buildings and gardens taken seriously in hand, and by this time many of the great pleasure gardens had vanished through ruin and neglect: hundreds, for instance, were lost to Kashmir.

The mausoleum itself stands on a simple platform, with four raised causeways leading outwards. A plan shows the arrangements for supplying water by underground pipes, but as so often today, the pools are dry. The charm of the site lies in the harmony between the pale colours of the tomb and the reflected light from the broad pearly river. So far as colour is concerned, this is probably the most sophisticated of all the Mughul gardens and its quality can be enjoyed to the full from the little river-gate.

So, from this family originated some remarkable buildings and gardens – the royal gardens of Kashmir, Asaf Khan's own Nishat Bagh, and above all, the Taj Mahal. For Ghiyas Beg's daughter and grand-daughter both became empresses, and it was to Mumtaz Mahal, Asaf Khan's daughter, that Shah Jahan raised the crowning glory of the Mughul era.

Detail of inlays in the interior. The dado is an entirely two-dimensional pattern: the inlays above show a considerable degree of realism.

The tombs, of yellow marble, contrast in their simplicity with the intricate marble lattice work, through which a diffused light reaches the interior.

WAH BAGH, HASSAN ABDAL, RAWALPINDI

'On Wednesday our encamping ground was Baba Hasan Abdal. . . . The most noted spot there is where a spring issues from the foot of the hill. . . . Khwaja Shamsu-d din Khwafi, who was for long the minister of my respected father, erected a small summer-house there, and excavated a cistern into which the water of the spring flows, supplying the fields and gardens with the means of irrigation.'

Memoirs of Jahangir

Near Hassan Abdal, where the road for Kashmir leaves the plains, is the site of ancient Taxila, where the Macedonian Alexander the Great was hospitably received after he had crossed the Indus in 326 B C. Here too is the old imperial camping-ground of the Mughuls, Wah Bagh. It is based, like so many, upon a spring at the foot of a hill. By tradition its name derives from Akbar who on first seeing the site exclaimed 'Wah Bagh!' (What a garden!), but the garden-palace itself was built later.

It was a place of considerable luxury, with a series of baths, proper heating and an ample water supply. Visitors in the nineteenth century described the interior as beautifully decorated with designs of flowers and vases in stucco work, while the floors were paved in yellow marble. Once while he was here, Jahangir tried his hand at fishing. He caught twelve fish, put pearls in their noses, and let them loose in the water. . . .

Wah Bagh: detail of the cascade.

Opposite: *Wah Bagh, Hassan Abdal.*

127

Mausoleum of Prince Khusrau's mother at Allahabad, Uttar Pradesh. Pencil and wash by Thomas and William Daniell, 1788–9.

KHUSRAU BAGH, ALLAHABAD

Jahangir's relations with his sons followed an erratic course. With Prince Khusrau they had been almost wholly tragic. Since he was popular and well loved, both Jahangir and his third son Prince Khurram (Shah Jahan) saw in him a threat to their own security and the prince's rebellion was put down with barbaric cruelty.

There is little doubt that his subsequent death was contrived by Shah Jahan and Asaf Khan, in whose custody he had been placed. Yet afterwards, Jahangir had his body disinterred, and brought down to Allahabad. On the way, each resting-place was marked by a shrine and a little garden was laid out around it. He is buried in the Khusrau Bagh, a terraced garden-tomb where he lies with his mother and sons.

THE LAKE PALACES, UDAIPUR

Looking down from the Maharana's palace upon Lake Pichola, two island palaces, Jagniwas and Jagmandir, seem to float like pearls upon the smooth water. On one of them, Jagmandir, Shah Jahan lived for a time when he too was in rebellion against his father. A domed pavilion, the Gul Mahal, was built about this period (1625–7) but the other buildings, though typically Mughul in silhouette, date from the eighteenth century. Each evening at dusk hundreds of green parakeets, wheeling and flashing in the setting sun, flock to the island and, with much squawking, settle for the night in the branches of the trees.

Udaipur. The Lake Palace, contemporary with the one on Jag Mandir.

Udaipur. Carved elephants at the Lake Palace on Jag Mandir where Shah Jahan, when a prince, took refuge from his father.

129

SHAHDARA, LAHORE

North-west of Lahore lies Nur Jahan's old pleasure garden, once known as the Dilkusha Garden. Here Jahangir visited during his lifetime, and here, after his death near Rajauri, he was buried. Nur Jahan designed his tomb, taking as her model the Tomb of I'timad-ud-Daula, her parents' burial-place at Agra.

The layout comprises firstly an outer *sarai* – courtyard; here travellers could once find shelter for the night in a series of alcoves round the walls. A tall gateway gives access to the inner garden, which contains the tomb. The enclosure is on a huge scale with fine interlocking patterns of raised causeways, canals and tanks, in which brick, traditional in Lahore, has been beautifully used. The tomb itself must have been intended to have a central dome, but whether this was never completed, or was subsequently destroyed, seems uncertain. Without it, the effect is a strange one, for the building seems too slight for the powerful layout leading up to it, and the minarets dominate where they should merely have supported. Round the base of the catafalque itself runs a charming and lifelike design of cyclamen and tulips, recalling Jahangir's beloved Kashmir.

Asaf Khan's tomb is close at hand, built by Shah Jahan in a favourite form, a dome surmounting an octagon. Nur Jahan herself lies in a bare and simple grave not far away. She wrote her own epitaph, which, translated by the poet John Bowen, runs thus:

> Upon my grave when I shall die,
> No lamp shall burn nor jasmin lie,
> No candle, with unsteady flame,
> Serve as reminder of my fame,
> No bulbul chanting overhead,
> Shall tell the world that I am dead.

Above: *Detail of the water channel running along the top of the retaining wall in the outer courtyard.*

Detail of chadar *from the central tank.*

Opposite: *Shahdara, Lahore: Jahangir's tomb. The star pattern of the causeway is in the brickwork traditional to Lahore.*

SHAH JAHAN 1628-1658

Prince Khurram had been more fortunate than his unhappy brother Khusrau. He commanded his father's armies with skill and success, and whilst still a prince, received the title of Shah Jahan. Like Akbar, Jahangir took his son travelling with him to Kashmir, and both made their contributions to the gardens at Shalamar and Vernag. On another occasion in India, Jahangir was clearly delighted by a splendid gift from his son:

'On Wednesday the 8th. I marched and halted on the 9th. The royal tent was pitched near a large tank. Shah Jahan presented me with a boat made in the Kashmir fashion, the sitting place of which they had made of silver. At the end of that day, I embarked in that boat and went round the tank.'

But the closing years of Jahangir's reign were marred by a rebellion organized by this much-loved son, though towards the end of the emperor's life some sort of reconciliation between them was effected.

After his accession, Shah Jahan maintained his interest in Kashmir. He visited it several times, and it is pleasant to read that on one occasion he ordered his troops to line the road on both sides, so that the royal procession should not trample down and damage the crops growing along the way. His own works in Kashmir were minor ones, but his son, Dara Shukoh, built two great gardens at Bijbehara and Peri Mahal. Meanwhile the emperor visited and planted trees on the Char Chenar Island on Lake Dal, and followed progress at the delightful little Chasma Shahi, the work of his comptroller and sometime governor in Kashmir, 'Ali Mardan Khan.

It was in India that Shah Jahan's true genius evolved, and it was directed primarily towards the cities of the Indian plains. In this, the circumstances of his birth and ancestry quite possibly played some part. Both his mother and grandmother had been Rajput princesses, so that Shah Jahan was more than half Rajput, and his Mongol forebears were receding into the past. The instinctive longings of the earlier emperors for the north, with its cooler climate and mountainous terrain, may well have been replaced by a real affinity with the great level plains, the strong sunlight and wide rivers of his mother's native land.

His major works are entirely urban and belong, indeed, more to the field of town planning than of landscape. Magnificent in scale,

Shah Jahan 'in my fortieth year'. Amongst the flowers, saffron, iris, tulip and daffodil are clearly seen. Other more hazardous identifications are hollyhock, campanula, lychnis, cranesbill and poppy.

شبه خوب جمال سالک منت علی اکبر

highly sophisticated in character, and executed with a wholly imperial disregard of cost, the city of Shahjahanabad at Delhi, the city-fort of Agra, the palaces and pavilions of Lahore and Ajmer, were primarily splendid settings for court life and for the spectacle and ceremonial of which it was composed. Even the mosques are designed as part of the total scene, for the Jami Masjid at Delhi, begun in Shah Jahan's reign, rises on its high platform to dominate the surrounding streets, while the Moti Masjid takes an important place in the fretted skyline of the Agra Fort.

To such a patron designers and craftsmen of the highest order were attracted. Builders of every kind, masons, jewellers, weavers, from Europe as well as Asia, were employed in tremendous numbers. Trade with Europe, too, was steadily developing, and in return for her textiles, dyes and spices, India was importing luxuries of every kind, above all silver, both for hoarding and for works of art. One of the emperor's most expensive treasures was the Peacock Throne. The name was derived from the two peacocks of the design, their widespread tails displaying every kind of precious stone, and between them a parrot, carved from a single emerald. In the eighteenth century the throne was plundered by Nadir Shah and subsequently broken up. Some fragments were inserted in the present Peacock Throne at Tehran. This was only one of some eleven such thrones belonging to Shah Jahan.

His love for his favourite wife has made him a romantic figure. Born Arjumand Banu Begam, daughter of Asaf Khan, niece of Nur Jahan, she received from Shah Jahan the title of Mumtaz Mahal, the 'Ornament of the Palace'. She bore him fourteen children and died in childbirth whilst travelling in the Deccan, for the emperor made no concessions to human frailty. In her memorial, the Taj Mahal, Mughul building reaches its peak. It took twenty-two years to build and it is said that Shah Jahan had intended to build himself another, in black marble, facing it across the Jumna. But towards the end of his life his health failed him, his character deteriorated, and in 1658 he was deposed by his son, Aurangzib, and imprisoned in the fort at Agra. Here he died, in 1666, seated in the pavilion near the Anguri Bagh, looking out over the river towards the Taj Mahal.

With him, the great tide of Mughul building came to its climax, and then subsided, for his successor was virtually uninterested in the arts. Looking back over five reigns, the ebb and flow of Persian influence can be traced throughout in both buildings and gardens. Babur's Ram Bagh, with its narrow water-courses; Humayun's tomb, with its intricate colour and pattern, its complexes of recessed arches, and the classical *char-bagh* of the garden, show Persian derivation at its most direct.

With Akbar the Indian-Rajput influence became more marked. Strong and forceful, with much use of red sandstone, his architecture had the robust character of fortress building, which indeed much of it was. Yet the tents and pavilions, in which so much of his active life was spent, threw back to Persia and Turkey, evoking the mosques and palaces of Isfahan. In painting and ornament, Hindu and even European influences began to react upon the formal Persian use of pattern and more and more realism developed in the decorative arts.

The contact with European painters was probably a factor in the appreciation of landscape as an art, as copies of European paintings began to circulate in India.

Jahangir, with nature his ruling passion, carried the process a step further. Painters under his patronage specialized in the lifelike presentation of birds, animals, and flowers. On one of the most accomplished, Ustad Mansur, he bestowed the title of the 'Marvel of the Age'. In his gardens, for the first time, nature became the dominant influence. Site and level, prospect and orientation, planting, and above all water in all its forms, from the reflective pool to the spectacular waterfall – these were the real constituents of the Kashmir gardens, to which the buildings were incidental. Jahangir was, in effect, the great exponent of the country homes of the Mughuls, while his son's interest lay in their city palaces.

Under Shah Jahan, there was a return to orthodoxy in all its aspects. The religious tolerance of his father and grandfather was replaced by a more consciously Muslim culture. It was less that the Hindus were oppressed, than that the Muslims were promoted as a ruling class, while the Jesuit missionaries did indeed actively suffer for a time. Foreign artists and craftsmen remained welcome, and Venetians and Turks in particular have left their mark upon the period.

Persian influence returned to building, as it did to policy: formality accorded well with the level sites of the plains. With it were allied the Indian tradition and an increasing use of white marble, to give the resulting buildings a repose and purity especially their own. Inlays of precious and semi-precious stones imposed their own discipline, realism gave way to a two-dimensional sense of pattern, in which the veining of cornelian, onyx, or topaz could be appreciated to the full.

Although many names of craftsmen and designers figure among the records of the time, there seems little doubt that it was Shah Jahan's own judgment and directing force which gave the achievements of his time their great quality. Perfect fusions of building and landscape are rare: the Taj Mahal and the Agra Fort are two which can hold their own with any in the world.

Dara Shukoh and Peri Mahal, Kashmir

Dara Shukoh, Shah Jahan's eldest son, was clearly intended by his father to succeed him, for he held all the privileges of the heir-apparent. He had good looks, intelligence, charm and courage in ample measure, but when the struggle for the succession with his brother Aurangzib began, he proved fatally incompetent, both as a military commander and in political manoeuvre.

In his youth all went well, and he played a leading part in court ceremonial. He married his cousin, Princess Nadira, and it was to her that he presented the superb collection of Mughul miniatures known as Dara Shukoh's Album. He had inherited his father's gift for splendour, his grandfather's love of nature, and he is remembered by two gardens in Kashmir. The first, at Bijbehara, was planned to extend on both sides of the Jhelum river. Traces have been found of

Peri Mahal. The ruined terrace.

the parterres and canals, but the garden fell into ruin, and is today marked only by the great chenars, and by the remains of a pavilion and a bridge. Clearly however the design was on a grand scale, reminiscent of the gardens of Delhi rather than those of Kashmir.

His other garden, near Srinagar, shows him to be the grandson of Jahangir. Peri Mahal, the Fairies' Palace, is on the hill immediately south-east of Lake Dal. There is a suggestion of a Greek temple in its siting, for it lies across a spur of rock, thrown into relief against the darker, higher mountains behind.

The façade, with a central building and flanking pavilions, is set upon a podium. Behind it, stepped terraces mount up the slope to a central climax, possibly once a dome. Five terraces can be seen, and traces of a number of fountains and tanks. It seems likely that the water was carried underground, for there appear to have been neither waterfalls nor canals. Now in ruins, remote and overgrown, Peri Mahal has the special magic of inaccessibility. The foreground is dramatic: white-stemmed poplars rise from the level lake shore, and, behind and above them, the Fairies' Palace seems to appear and disappear as the light strikes or leaves the walls.

It was built supposedly as a school of astrology for Dara Shukoh's tutor, Akhund Mullah Shah. Astronomy and astrology had been linked for centuries, and astrologers had always held important and responsible positions in the Mughul courts. Babur described the observatories of Samarkand in detail, while Humayun, of all the emperors, was perhaps the most deeply influenced; he is even said to have dressed in the colours appropriate to the planets. Akbar's astrologers, consulted on his campaign in Kashmir, had justified his faith in them, while Jahangir, too, often refers to the success of his own Jotik Ray in forecasting the future. Throughout Asia, wrote François Bernier, astrologers are consulted on every particular, in the belief that every action in life is predestined by the stars. A belief not without its followers today.

Inside Peri Mahal: a water-colour by Mary Popham Blyth, who accompanied her clergyman brother in 1868 to Kashmir and camped in the ruins (probably quite a usual practice among Europeans).

Left: Peri Mahal, set on a spur of the Zebanwan mountain overlooking Lake Dal; below, miniature of Dara Shukoh.

Chasma Shahi.
As at Achabal, the pavilions are Kashmiri, but built on Mughul bases.

CHASMA SHAHI – THE ROYAL SPRING, KASHMIR

Built in 1632, an early inscription at the gateway attributes this garden to Shah Jahan himself. It seems more likely that the actual builder was 'Ali Mardan Khan, working to the emperor's instructions. In its present form, the garden combines the work of many hands and various periods.

The original garden was small, strongly axial and closely moulded to the contours of the mountain. The design derived from a powerful spring at the top of the garden, renowned for the excellence of its water, which bubbled up through a marble lotus basin, now vanished, set in the floor of the upper pavilion. From here the flow was led down, by way of a little cascade and a canal, to fill a wide rectangular tank, with a single jet. Here was reflected the second and principal pavilion, standing on a magnificent retaining wall some twenty feet high. Below, a second chute dropped sharply down the centre of the wall to feed another water garden at the lower level.

The composition is a miniature one, yet tremendously effective in its bold use of level. The main pavilion in particular has an enchanting site. On one side the outlook is cloistered, intimate; the pool, canal and upper pavilion are part of a private world. On the other, there is the drop of the retaining wall and a spectacular view over Lake Dal.

The garden as a whole has been much extended and restored and today, with dramatic changes of level, rich planting and an unusual measure of asymmetry, it is strongly evocative of both Italian Renaissance and English Tudor gardens. The Mughul work is to be

The garden is set close in to the mountain side.

Below, left: The main pavilion: water from the spring runs through the pavilion and ripples down a patterned chadar *into a square pool.*

Detail of the chadar.

seen in the cascades, the plinths of the two pavilions, and the complex of canals, tanks and fountains. The two pavilions themselves are Kashmiri and the upper garden has been widened into a broad terrace, while at the lower level an extensive flower garden has been developed. The approach is by way of a steep flight of steps, culminating in an arch, which is the present entrance to the lowest water garden. It is probable that these too were not original, but they have a force and character which contribute greatly to the whole design.

Easily accessible from Srinagar, Chasma Shahi is always full of visitors, for its charm lies perhaps less in the details of historical interest than in the romantic atmosphere that the whole evokes. It is a garden for the late afternoon and evening: for the panorama, from the upper terrace, of Lake Dal in the setting sun, with its background of hills, and the clear and beautiful details of the two islands, the bridges and the bunds, seen either from the terrace, or through the lattices of the main pavilion, remains unforgettable. The sharp contrast, too, between the bare mountainside beyond and the luxuriance within, with its clipped trees looking oddly Elizabethan and its riot of colour, can reconcile even the purist to its historical irrelevance. Then there are the birds, tame and lazy, in the windows of the pavilion, and the striped Persian roses in the modern garden below as a reminder of the entirely different scale of planting which these gardens must once have known.

Miniature of ʿAli Mardan Khan. An outstanding governor of Kashmir, he built a number of fine sarais or rest-houses along the Pir Panjal route from India to Kashmir. He was a Persian and had been Governor of Kandahar under Shah Safi. Here, apparently, he had been ill-used, and he surrendered the city to Shah Jahan, subsequently going to work for him at Delhi. A capable administrator, he became, as it were, Comptroller of Works. In this capacity he was responsible for a number of notable projects, in particular the canals bringing water to the Red Fort at Delhi and the Shalamar Bagh at Lahore.

COLOUR PLATES (pp. 141–3)
Chasma Shahi, Lake Dal. The entrance garden seen from the main pavilion.

Akbar's tomb, Sikandra. Looking across the plain towards the river Jumna.

Rustum, a Persian hero, with his mistress in a garden: a Mughul interpretation, c. 1565, of Persian design.

The Moti Masjid, or Pearl Mosque, in the Red Fort at Delhi. White marble enclosed in red sandstone, as at the Taj Mahal, was a frequent Mughul concept.

Pan-Chakki, Aurangabad.

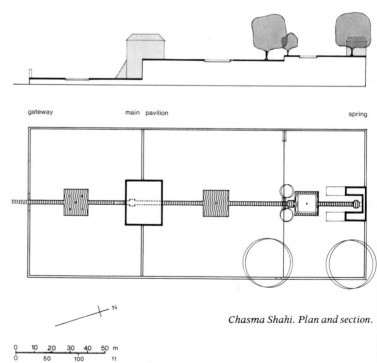

gateway   main pavilion   spring

Chasma Shahi. Plan and section.

140

The Island of the Four Chenars, Kashmir

The two islands in Lake Dal, the Rupa-Lank and the Sona-Lank (the silver and the golden Lanka) are of considerable antiquity. Entirely artificial, their early names derive from a tradition that silver was buried upon the one and gold on the other. The northern island (the Sona-Lank) in particular has been for centuries an irresistible attraction to travellers. Lying midway across the lake, it is a mere half-acre in size, with carefully squared boundaries. It lies just above the water level, so that the trees seem to be floating in the water. The present name, the Char Chenar, dates from Shah Jahan's visit, when he planted a plane tree symmetrically in each corner.

From nineteenth-century accounts it is possible to trace the changes which have arisen from time to time. Victor Jacquemont landed there in 1831; only two trees, he noted had then survived. Soon after, there is a description from Baron Huegel and G. T. Vigne, who were in Kashmir together. It mentions a central building, with marble pillars and a little tower, set in a garden filled with roses, stocks, marigolds and vines. Under one of the plane trees was a fine water-wheel, of Himalayan cedar, which lifted water from the lake to irrigate the garden. Today all these have vanished, to be replaced by four small pavilions. There are three chenars; the island cries out for the fourth to be replanted.

The Char Chenar, Lake Dal, Kashmir, as it is today. The island is entirely artificial and was probably constructed by King Zain-ul-Abidin in the 15th century.

COLOUR PLATE
Spring flowers from Dara Shukoh's Album.

145

A drawing by G. T. Vigne, about 1832. The silhouette of the little tower suggests that the building dated from Mughul times. According to Vigne, the roof was once covered with silver.

It is a place purely for delight: for solitary contemplation of the mountains and water, or for revelry and the company of friends. The possibilities are dramatically illustrated by an evening recorded in about 1830. Kripa Ram, the Governor of Kashmir, was enjoying a festival upon the island. Boats crowded it round; there was feasting, there were dancing girls, and, as the climax, a splendid display of fireworks was set off, while guns thundered from the Fort. Suddenly the king's envoy landed, summoning the governor at once to Lahore and brooking no delay. Kripa Ram left at the height of the festivities, never to return, instead to be disgraced and dismissed, his enemies having brought about his downfall.

SHALAMAR BAGH, DELHI

Lying to the north-west of Shahjahanabad, close by the Grand Trunk road near Badli Sarai, was once yet another great pleasure garden, comparable to those of the same name at Lahore and Srinagar. It was laid out by one of Shah Jahan's favourite wives, A'Azzu-un-Nisa, and evidently the Shalamar Bagh in Kashmir had been her inspiration. Its remains are recorded in a plan showing a garden of considerable size, its main feature being a central canal about eighteen feet wide, which ran the full length of the garden. According to a contemporary historian, Muhammad Salih, it was originally even larger.

The upper terrace stood some nine feet above the lower, and at the change of level was a complex of tanks and buildings, with 'rows of pearl showering fountains', and 'marvellously adorned halls'. Some distance below lay an octagonal reservoir, similar to that at Vernag, and, from the records, it would seem that this reservoir originally marked the middle of the garden, with a third and even larger terrace below it.

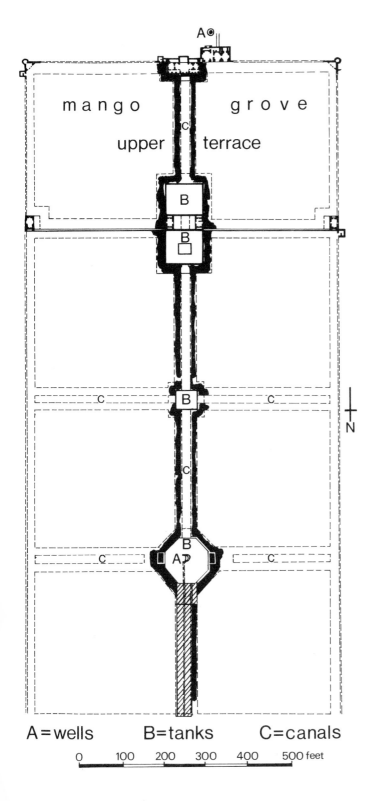

A●

m a n g o   g r o v e

upper   terrace

C

B

B

C   B   C

N

C

B
A

C   C

A = wells   B = tanks   C = canals

0   100   200   300   400   500 feet

Shalamar Bagh, Delhi. A plan of the remains, prepared by the ARCHAEOLOGICAL SURVEY OF INDIA *in 1903. Minor canals cross the principal one.*

147

It took four years to build, and was opened ceremonially by the emperor in September 1650, the occasion being marked by a festival. Bernier, visiting it, described it as regal and beautiful, but a mere shadow of Fontainebleau or Versailles. It was to figure notably in the reign of Aurangzib, but later fell into ruin and decay. It played its part in the downfall of the Mughul Empire, for during March 1739 the Persian Nadir Shah camped there, a prelude to the massacre of Delhi and the seizure of the Peacock Throne. By the end of the eighteenth century much had already been destroyed, and the most valuable materials plundered. Today few people are aware even of its location.

SHALAMAR BAGH, LAHORE

The Shalamar gardens at Lahore were laid out by 'Ali Mardan Khan, on Shah Jahan's instructions. The first great undertaking had been the construction of a canal to bring the waters of the Ravi river up to the gardens in Lahore. By 1633 the canal was ready and Shah Jahan celebrated its completion by giving instructions for the creation of a garden on a grand scale, with tanks and fountains, a bath-house and several pavilions. About 1642 the work was complete and he paid the garden a ceremonial visit, after consultations with his astrologers as to an auspicious date.

One of the two parterres to east and west of the central reservoir. The parterres are similar in design and proportion to those at the Taj Mahal, but the detail of the pattern is floral rather than star-shaped.

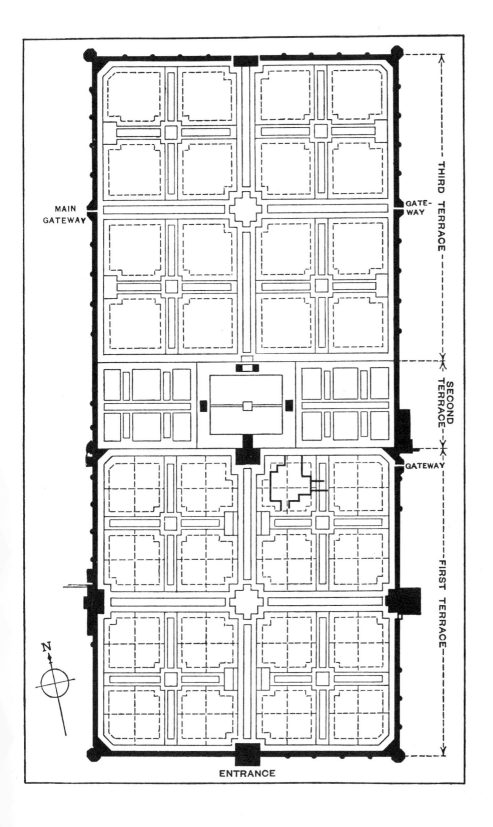

MAIN
GATEWAY

GATE-
WAY

THIRD TERRACE

SECOND TERRACE

GATEWAY

FIRST TERRACE

N

ENTRANCE

The view from the zenana terrace. In the foreground is the emperor's marble throne, set in shallow water and looking out across the great tank which is said to have had 152 fountains. Water from the tank passes between the two pavilions to cascade down on to the lowest terrace.

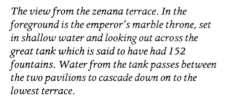

The design comprises three terraces, dropping down from the south, the changes in level being about fifteen feet. The first and third terraces are *char-baghs* of similar proportion and design; the middle one contains the great reservoir which is the principal feature of the garden. There are conflicting records as to whether the layout was once much larger. Some writers claim that there were originally seven terraces, corresponding with the seven degrees of Paradise, but others consider the present garden as complete in itself. As it is of considerable size and surrounded by a high brick wall, this seems the more probable. The order of entering the garden, however, has been transposed, for the original entrance was to the lowest terrace. This was customary in Mughul gardens, so that the progress was upwards, with the cascades facing the visitor and new delights revealed as each terrace was surmounted until the last, wholly private, zenana terrace was reached. (Fadai Khan's Pinjaur gardens were one of the few exceptions to this rule.) The upper terrace at Lahore was known as the Farah Baksh (the Bestower of Pleasure), while the middle and lower terraces, forming the more public part of the garden, were known together as the Faiz Baksh (the Bestower of Plenty). 'Ali Mardan Khan, as a former governor of Kashmir, was likely to have been familiar with the Shalamar garden there, which had received similar names.

Shalamar Bagh, Lahore. The top terrace, formerly the zenana garden. The balcony of the pavilion at the end of the central canal overlooks the two lower terraces.

Detail of the surround to the central reservoir.

151

Shalamar Bagh, Lahore.
The water flows down from the pavilion on the
zenana terrace by way of a carved marble
chadar *or water chute. At the base,*
overhanging the water, is the emperor's
throne with its low, carved balustrade – a
convenient height when sitting. The fountain
jet between the water chute and the throne,
carved to resemble a lotus, is believed to be
original.

It is the central level, however, which is the most spectacular. The great reservoir, over two hundred feet across, once contained a hundred and fifty-two fountains, of which over a hundred remain. In the centre is a marble platform, reached by a narrow causeway. The water flows down through the southern pavilion by way of a broad carved marble chute or *chadar* and at the bottom, overhanging the water, is the emperor's throne of white marble, where he could sit to watch the fountains play, the hot air always cooled by the rush of water.

Round the whole reservoir runs a double paved path, with a flower parterre. Much of the paving, as at Shahdara, is in the brickwork traditional to Lahore. The planting of the garden must have seen many changes. Shah Jahan himself is said to have ordered fruit trees from Kabul and Kandahar. Historians refer to continuous flower-beds, with plane trees and aspens at intervals, and the emperor is recorded as having himself planted an aspen between two planes. Under the trees were grass platforms for comfortable reclining in the shade. The original plantings included: mango, cherry, apricot, peach, plum, apple, almond, quince, seedless mulberry, sour orange, sweet orange and cypress, together with aromatic plants.

Abdul Hamid Lahori describes the cascades, with innumerable *chini-kanas*, or pigeon holes, beneath them, in which were placed golden vases of flowers by day and camphorated wax candles at night. The original number of fountains has been estimated at four hundred and fifty, many of which still survive. In the canals, the water is thrown up in jets twelve feet high.

The buildings, too, were of intricate design and beautiful work-manship, and the garden seems to have been especially noted for the large number of buildings which it contained. There were four main pavilions on the zenana terrace, with minor ones in the four corners, together with four more on the central level, of which two were paired on the north side. There was also a *hummum*, or bath suite, on the east, with hot and cold baths and a dressing-room, while on the lowest terrace, facing up the central axis of the garden, was the hall of private audience. The garden seems, indeed, to have been used as a royal camping ground, for whenever the emperor visited Lahore, it is said that the number of buildings made it unnecessary for tents to be pitched. Aurangzib too, in 1655, spent some time encamped in the gardens, waiting for his astrologers to decide the most fortunate moment to enter the city. This very availability of buildings has been a factor in their decline, since their convenience offered an attraction to successive generations of campaigning troops.

The pavilions were stripped of their marble and agate work by the Sikhs in the eighteenth century, to decorate the Ram Bagh and Golden Temple at Amritsar. The present pavilions are restorations in brick and plaster, and comparatively little of the original work survives.

LAHORE FORT

'All these palaces (Delhi, Agra and Lahore) are full of gardens with running water, which flows in channels into reservoirs of stone, jasper and marble. In all the rooms and halls of these palaces there are ordinarily fountains or reservoirs of the same stone of pro-portionate size. In the gardens of these palaces there are always flowers according to the season. There are no large fruit trees of any sort, in order not to hinder the delight of the open view. In these palaces are seats and private rooms, some of which are in the midst of the running water. In the water are many fish for delight.'

Niccolao Manucci

The Fort at Lahore is one of three great Mughul palace-forts. Here Akbar, Jahangir, Shah Jahan and Aurangzib made their contributions, but it is much changed by time. Two gardens survive here in recognizable form: Jahangir's Quadrangle, and the Paien Bagh or zenana garden.

Jahangir's Quadrangle (1617–18) is a large open space with a central reservoir containing fountains and a marble platform reached by a causeway. The surrounding grass areas are dished for irrigation, but no trace remains of the original planting.

The Paien Bagh is more intimate in scale, with paths paved in a hexagonal pattern of red brick. Here the ladies of the harem could walk daily and enjoy the fruit and fragrance which were the theme of the garden. A brick platform and water tank are set in the centre. To either side are smaller grassy subdivisions, with shallow reflecting pools and small orange trees. The plots were once enclosed by red sandstone railings, of which an original example still stands in another part of the fort.

It was from Lahore that William Finch of the East India Company gave one of the most detailed descriptions of actual flower and fruit planting that has come down to us:

'. . . adjoining to this is a garden of the King's in which are very good apples, but small, toot [tut-mulberry], white and red, almonds, peaches, figges, grapes, quinces, orenges, limmons, pomgranates, stock-gellow flowers [the white stock, *Mathiola incana*], marigolds, wall-flowers, ireos [the Florentine iris], pinkes white and red, with divers sorts of Indian flowers.'

Lahore Fort. Jahangir's quadrangle.

Opposite, top: *Detail of a Mughul red sandstone balustrade. Similar balustrades were probably used in the Paien Bagh in Lahore Fort.* Below: *The Paien Bagh or Ladies' Garden.*

Detail of the hexagonal red brick paving.

155

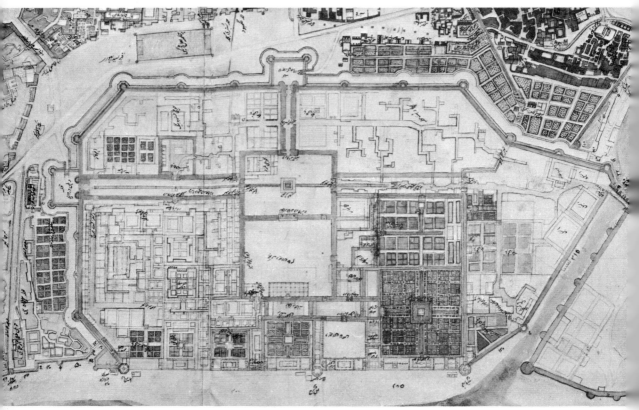

156

The west wall, with Aurangzib's gateway.

THE RED FORT, DELHI

Named after its builder, Shahjahanabad was perhaps the finest of the succession of cities which have been built at Delhi. Bernier, describing Shah Jahan's decision to develop a new city at Delhi, says that the emperor considered the summer heat and humidity of Agra made it unsuitable for his capital.

A conscious effort of the imagination is needed to picture the Red Fort as it must have appeared at the height of its splendour.

The Fort itself, immense as it is, was only a part of the whole planned complex. Enclosed on three sides by walls, on the fourth it was open to the Jumna river, then spanned only by a bridge of boats. It was here, on a terrace some two thousand feet long, that the principal buildings of the palace were sited. Between this terrace and the river lay a long sandy space for the staging of every kind of spectacle, particularly the elephant fights of which many vivid descriptions abound.

Two main gates gave entrance to the Fort, the Lahore gate on the west, the Delhi gate on the south. In Bernier's time the walls, except on the river side, were encircled by a moat filled with water and well stocked with fish. Beyond this lay gardens and the royal square, so that the whole vast red wall was set off by the rich colours of flowers and trees. Centred on the Lahore gate was the Chandni Chauk, the main street of the city, with trees and a canal of running water, forming an introduction to the palace in which irrigation played a vital part.

While the Red Fort remains impressive, it is lacking today in this element of water, which the Mughuls prized above all. Bernier describes the city within the Fort:

The Red Fort, Delhi.
Opposite, above: *A painting of the Fort from the river side, from a Persian manuscript. The present day view corresponds very closely.*

Below: *A plan dated 1850 shows the moat and gardens which once existed outside the Fort. At bottom right may be seen the original lay-out of the Hayat Baksh garden. Little more than half has survived, so that the central pavilion now appears to flank the design.*

The Red Fort, Delhi.
This was once one of four central canals of
the Hayat Baksh garden, where the hyacinths,
says Fadil Khan, 'made the earth the envy of
the sky'. It ends in the Bhadon pavilion.

A side view of the Bhadon pavilion, showing
the massive water tanks built up at the back.

'After you have passed this Gate, you find a long and large Street, divided into two by a Channel of running Water . . . The Water of the Channel runneth dividing itself through the whole Seraglio, and at length falleth into Ditches to fill them.'

'To provide the water, an existing canal, built by Sultan Firuz Shah Khulji, taking water off the Jumna near Khizrabad, was repaired. A new channel was constructed by 'Ali Mardan Khan to connect it with Delhi, cut with great labour through fields and rocky ground.'

All this has vanished; the Chandni Chauk canal has been filled in, the moat and gardens are replaced by a stretch of grass. Aurangzib's great entrance barbican outside the Lahore gate is somehow a barrier to the sense of arrival and within the Fort about half of the old enchanting city has been replaced by barracks and official buildings.

The palaces themselves have been sympathetically and beautifully restored and the grass and trees that surround them are pleasant enough, until one begins to read the old accounts and to realize what has been lost. In one of his most evocative passages, Bernier describes the mosaic of private apartments, houses and galleries:

'There is almost no Chamber but it hath at its Door a Storehouse of running water; that 'tis full of Parterres, pleasant Walks, shady Places, Rivolets, Fountains, Jets of Water, Grotta's, great Caves against the heat of the day, and great Terrasses raised high, and very airy, to sleep upon in the cool: in a word, you know not there what 'tis to be hot.'

There were two major gardens, the Hayat Baksh or Life-giving Garden, and the Mahtab Bagh or Moonlight Garden, combined to form one grand design. The latter no longer exists, but much of the Hayat Baksh remains. Designed as a water garden, the central pavilion stood in a pool full of fountains. From this ran four canals, which terminated at south and north in small water pavilions, the Sawan and the Bhadon. These names are linked with the months of July and August, when the ladies sat in the pavilion of the month, to enjoy the prevailing breeze. At Udaipur, the same names also recall a tradition of rainfall. In Sawan (July) there falls a lighter rain, while Bhadon (August) brings a torrential downpour. The fountains round the Lotus Pool at Udaipur can be varied to simulate light or heavy rain.

Zafar Mahal, built by Bahadur Shah II in the mid-19th century. The tank of red sandstone was originally the centre of the Hayat Baksh garden and was intended for bathing. The pavilion has since been restored but the tank is no longer filled with water. Some restoration of the water would greatly enhance the interior of the Fort.

On the river side the wall of the Red Fort, with the private apartments, overlooks the flat meadow where elephant fights were staged and troops passed in review. The Shah Burj pavilion is on the right, the domes of the Moti Masjid may be seen in the centre.

Along the terrace to the river was a water parterre, terminating in the beautiful little Shah-Burj pavilion, with its own fountain and water chute. The details throughout were fantastic. Each of the canals had three rows of fountains, while the central pool had no less than forty-nine fountains inside and a hundred and twelve on the four sides. Each was plated with silver. Waterfalls fell from the pavilions, and in the arch-shaped niches below them, gold and silver pots were placed, containing silver flowers by day and candles by night. Richly planted, the colours of the Hayat Baksh were predominantly crimson and purple and the scent pervaded the garden. The Mahtab Bagh, by contrast, was planted with pale flowers only, jasmine, tuberoses, lilies and narcissus, while both gardens were enclosed by rows of cypresses.

The Fort was begun in 1639, with Shah Jahan naturally consulting astrologers at its inception. It took some nine years to complete, and the emperor's first entrance was marked with splendid ceremony, with Dara Shukoh showering his father with silver and gold. From below the great terrace, there seems to be little change, the series of beautiful buildings still delicately poised along the skyline. Here the emperor appeared daily at dawn to his people gathered on the river bank below and here, in the Diwan-i-Khas, the Hall of Private Audience, stood his Peacock Throne. The same inscription appears as at Shalamar, and at its zenith, the Red Fort at Delhi must indeed have seemed a paradise on earth.

The Diwan-i-Khas, or Hall of Private Audience, seen from the Rang Mahal. In the foreground is the marble water-course which runs right through the private apartments.

The water parterre in front of the Shah-Burj pavilion. Remnants of this stone pattern were found beneath layers of rubbish when the gardens were restored at the beginning of this century.

The red sandstone outer walls, built by Akbar in 1565.

THE FORT, AGRA

'To the Dersane Gate at the hour when the brilliant rays of Phoebus quit Western shores and seek to illuminate and gladden Eastern lands, the Emperor (Shah Jahan) sallies forth daily. In this square the gentlemen of his Court are already waiting to salute him and give him the morning's greeting with the customary Tassalima. . . .'

The Travels of Sebastien Manrique

The Fort at Agra was one of Akbar's first great fortress constructions and the outer walls of red sandstone remain to the present day. Internally, there were once numbers of buildings in the same red stone, but many were demolished by Shah Jahan, who replaced them by a superb series of marble palaces and mosques.

The Agra Fort has suffered less than its counterpart at Delhi from the depredations of time. A level site is always more vulnerable to change, whereas at Agra the towering walls and ramped approaches have stood impervious even to the military. Changes of level provide constant surprises: new views open, sometimes contained and secret, sometimes broad and calm, until the eastern terraces are reached, with their incomparable prospect across the river to the Taj Mahal. It is this quality which has enabled the Fort to sustain the loss of its internal gardens and pools. The buildings are visually exciting in their relationship to one another and at the last there are the wide stretches of the river to compensate for the lack of water within the walls.

The two principal gardens were the Machchi Bhawan, or Fish Square; and the Anguri Bagh, or Grape Garden. The Machchi

From the Jasmine Tower, where he was held prisoner, Shah Jahan could gaze across at the Taj Mahal.

The Machchi Bhawan, or Fish Square. Originally laid out with geometric flower beds, fountains, water channels and tanks containing the sacred fish, it was pillaged by the Jats in the 18th century.

The Khas Mahal, or Private Palace, seen across the raised marble tank in the centre of the Anguri Bagh. The soil for this garden is said to have been brought from Kashmir.

A side entrance, through marble walls, to the Anguri Bagh, or Grape Garden, in the zenana quarters of the Fort.

Bhawan owes its name to the pools of sacred fish which it once contained. When the Jats of Bharatpur ransacked the Fort in the eighteenth century, they carried off many of the marble fountains and tanks to decorate Suraj Mal's own garden at Deeg, and the Fish Square today is represented only by a rectangle of grass. Yet the prospect is architecturally so distinguished, with the domes of the Moti Masjid appearing above the two-storeyed cloister, and with its sunlit terrace on the east, that the loss seems negligible.

The Fort is a succession of such groupings, and a potent reminder that landscape does not need planting to be memorable. Spaciousness and enclosure, sunlight and shadow, buildings and river, and the misty spaces of the plain beyond, together combine to make a landscape design of the finest quality.

The other garden, the Anguri Bagh, is a complete contrast. The private garden of the zenana quarter, it lies open and level and sunny: a traditional Mughul garden. The name more probably derives from the decorative pattern of vines inlaid on the buildings near by, than from the use of the garden to grow grapes, though a stone pergola once existed. Tavernier, the jeweller, wrote: 'Before the Divan is a Gallery, that serves for a Portico; which Cha-Jean had a design to have adorn'd all over with a kind of Latice-work of Emraulds and Rubies that should have represented to the life Grapes when they are green, and when they begin to grow red. But this design which made such a noise in the World, and requir'd more

Riches, than all the World could afford to perfect, remains un-finish'd; there being only three Stocks of a Vine in Gold, with their leaves, as the rest ought to have been; and enamel'd in their natural colours, with Emraulds, Rubies and Granates wrought into the fashion of Grapes.'

When the garden was restored, on the instructions of Lord Curzon, many disfiguring accretions were cleared away. Today, the intri-cately patterned parterres show little of the luxuriance they had in Mughul times, while the garden's finest features, the big reservoir reflecting the Khas Mahal, and the marble waterfall below it, lie empty and dazzlingly white in the sun.

Shah Jahan was to know the Fort in many aspects. Here was celebrated the marriage feast of his two sons, Dara Shukoh and Sultan Suja, when the future still seemed bright before them. It was a festival of fireworks and light, as Peter Mundy relates:

'First a ranck of great Eliphants, whose bellies were full of squibbs, Crackers, etts. Then a ranck of Gyants with wheeles in their hands, then a ranck of Monsters, then of Turrets, then of Artificiall trees . . . all full of Rocketts. . . . Also I think there were noe less then a million of lights burninge in the meane tyme, as Characks [*chiragh*,

A detail of the marble fountain pool in front of the Khas Mahal.

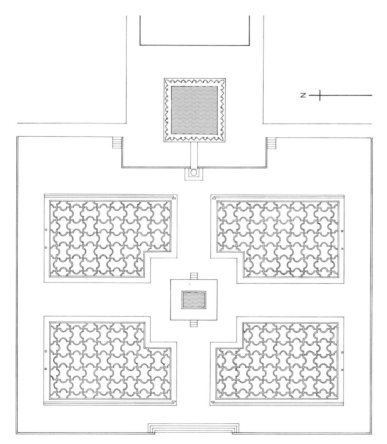

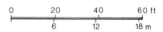

Plan. The Anguri Bagh was the garden of the zenana quarter. The north pavilion is said to have been occupied by Roshanara Begam, while Jahanara, who remained with her father during his imprisonment, occupied the south side.

165

Above: *Anguri Bagh. Red sandstone rings in the walls at first-floor level, like those at Sikandra, were used to stretch coverings over the garden.*

Right: *The marble cascade: by day, gold and silver vases filled with gold flowers were set in the niches behind the water. At night the vases were replaced by lights.*

an earthen lamp], Lanthornes, Lampes, etts. fastned and placed in rancks one above another on the Castle wall, with turretts etts. edifices, in a manner clean Covered with them from the ground to the Topp, vizt 3 or 4 rancks of small and a ranck of great lights, and then small and then great againe; also a great part of the plaine covered with Lamps.'

Almost daily there was some public spectacle; fights between lions, elephants, tigers and other animals; on Thursdays, a grimmer day, the sentences of the condemned were carried out. Both at Agra and Delhi were terrains especially devoted to elephant fighting. In each case, these were beside the river, since the infuriated beasts could frequently only be brought under control at the end by being driven into the water. The emperor and his court could watch from above, the common people from below. The fights took place between pairs of combat elephants, each with two riders. The animals fought one another across a mud wall, and the victor was he who finally demolished the wall and routed his opponent. It was the riders who suffered most, being frequently trampled to death in the *mêlée*. They took a formal farewell of their wives and families the night before: if they won, the prize-money was good; if they died, the emperor provided for their wives and children.

At the end of a lifetime of action and splendour came the years of imprisonment. Yet, by the standards of the time, the terms of this were fairly lenient. Shah Jahan's captivity amounted to what today would be called house arrest. He had a suite of rooms in the Fort, the company of his daughter Jahanara, and his collection of jewels. Aurangzib corresponded with, but did not visit him. He was buried in the Taj Mahal, but there were those who considered his funeral ceremonies to have been unduly scamped.

On the other side of the world, within the decade, some parallel to Aurangzib's puritanism might be seen in Cromwell, and he, after all, beheaded his opponent.

THE TAJ MAHAL, AGRA

The Taj Mahal, like the Venus de Milo, is so familiar through endless reproductions that to see it in fact comes as a surprise. The well-known view is there: the canal, the cypresses, and at the end of the vista a building that transcends all criticism, that is not less perfect than had been expected, but more. Yet this very reputation has left one unprepared to find the mausoleum itself the climax of a layout of remarkable beauty and complexity.

Shah Jahan's memorial to his best-loved wife took twenty-two years to build (1632–54). Legend has it that Mumtaz Mahal herself had previously chosen the site as the result of a dream. She died following the birth of her fourteenth child, and the following year, work on the tomb began. Her body, brought back to Agra, was buried temporarily in the gardens, until the actual sepulchre should be ready.

Tavernier describes how he himself saw both the commencement and the completion of the work, and that about twenty thousand workmen were employed throughout the whole period of building. He records, too, Shah Jahan's intention to build himself a second tomb:

'Chah-jehan had begun to raise his own Monument on the other side of the River, but the wars with his Son, broke off that design, nor did Aurangzib, now reigning, ever take any care to finish it.'

The second memorial was apparently intended in black marble, with a bridge to join the two. Dara Shukoh's garden at Bijbehara in Kashmir was based on just such a concept but at Agra one may well feel grateful that the project was never carried out, for to add to the design would surely have been to diminish it.

A small city was set up on the approaches to the Taj Mahal. Here there were streets of shops, buildings, and *sarais* where merchants and shopkeepers followed their trades. The revenue which this produced was available for the upkeep of the memorial, just as in smaller gardens the fruit plantations had served a similar purpose. Peter Mundy refers to the area as Tage Gunge, while a nineteenth-century plan calls it 'Momtazabad in Ruins'. This plan, usually known as Colonel Hodgson's plan, provides a complete record of the whole complex. Prepared in the Surveyor-General's office in India, and dated 1828, the detail and drawing are of the highest order. A

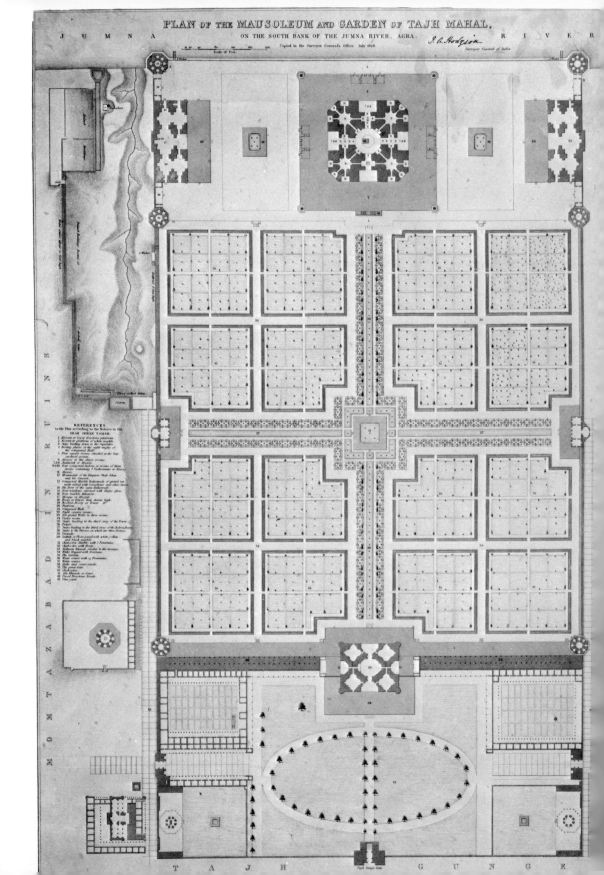

PLAN OF THE MAUSOLEUM AND GARDEN OF TAJH MAHAL,
ON THE SOUTH BANK OF THE JUMNA RIVER, AGRA.

J. A. Hodgson
Surveyor General of India

Copied in the Surveyor General's Office. July 1828.

Scale of Feet.

J U M N A

R I V E R

M O M T A Z A B A D   I N   R U I N S

T A J H   G U N G E

Tajh Gunge Gate.

tribute to its long-dead makers is due; to Colonel Hodgson himself; to Burke and James and Winston the surveyors, measuring the gardens and plotting the trees; and to Peeareedaul and Biswass, whose draughtsmanship and calligraphy have produced a minor work of art.

In one respect the layout echoes that of the Red Fort at Delhi, an immense enclosure, walled on three sides, with the fourth open to the river. The levels are deceptive, for the calm regularity of the interior leaves one unprepared for the drop in levels to the river. For even upon the approaches, Shah Jahan had ordered the ground levels to be changed 'cawseinge hills to be made level because they might not hinder the prospect of it.'

Once arrived at the main entrance courtyard, the great red sandstone gatehouse gives access to the garden. Bernier describes this at great length, feeling 'the edifice has a magnificent appearance'.

Top: *The Taj seen within its outer matrix of red sandstone.*

Above: *The battlements to the garden walk around the top of the enclosing wall, restored in 1903 on the directions of Lord Curzon. According to the official Survey, 'each crenellation is inlaid with a floral pattern in white marble, with a black marble centre; this occurs both on the outside and inside of the wall, while on the inside there is also a band of inlaid white marble extending the whole length of the wall below the crenellations.'*

Opposite: *The Taj Mahal, Agra. Layout plan, prepared in 1828 by the Surveyor-General of India, Colonel Hodgson.*

The river terraces of the Taj with black and white ripple paving. In the distance is the Fort.

From the archway within, the Taj Mahal itself first appears. Many writers have referred to it as 'floating', and perhaps no other word so well describes this building: changing under every changing light, yet always with this strange ethereal quality, as of something just alighted upon the earth, rather than raised from it by the labour of twenty-two years.

The garden facing the entrance is again a classical *char-bagh* but with one major departure from the generality of Mughul tomb plans. The building itself is placed, not at the centre as at, for example, Sikandra, but at the end of the garden on a raised terrace to form the climax of the whole design. The recurrent Mughul colour concept, the white marble jewel within its red sandstone casket, is nowhere so perfectly illustrated as here. The tomb, not only white, but actually glittering with semi-precious stones, is flanked by two red

At each end of the cross axis is a pavilion in red sandstone, built into the boundary wall.

sandstone buildings, the one a mosque, the other an assembly hall. Four smaller octagonal pavilions mark the corners of the river platform: the retaining walls and the flagged paths of the garden itself are all in degrees of red, completing the theme. Arriving at the tomb, the last and loveliest of the disclosures becomes apparent: the setting on the wide curve of the Jumna, with the plunging depth of the retaining wall below and in the distance, across the water, the crenellated outline of the Fort, the domes of the Moti Masjid glittering and all the smoky tones of Agra city beyond. The tomb itself stands on a handsome platform, the ripple design of which is symbolic of the water in which it would normally have been set.

The proportions of the garden have been much altered by the Europeanized planting of the last century. The 'four-fold field plot' has been transformed by the planting of large specimen trees into

From the first floor of the entrance gateway. The red sandstone building to the left of the Taj is a mosque. Distinguished pilgrims were made welcome in the building on the right.

A frieze of flowers on the base of the outside walls of the Taj. Tulips and an iris are clearly seen on the left and at the centre, but the plant on the right would seem to be imaginary, although the actual flower bears a strong resemblance to the Dillenia shown on page 191.

an avenue, forcing the perspective towards the tomb, so that much of the detailed layout in the rest of the garden goes unseen and unvisited. The enclosure was almost certainly originally planted with fruit trees, with taller trees for shady walks at either side, and the causeways, as in Mughul gardens generally, are slightly raised to allow for irrigation. Bernier refers too to 'many parterres full of flowers', which no longer exist. At the centre of the garden is a fine raised tank, reflecting the tomb as in a mirror image, and on the cross axes stand two more not inconsiderable pavilions in red sandstone. To the south is the cloister of the garden entrance, and here the poor were admitted three times a week in the rainy season to receive the emperor's charity.

Many details of great subtlety arise. The star-shaped pattern of the parterres is preserved along the main canal; the inscription round the central arch of the tomb is graduated so that the effect of perspective is offset and the letters read as of equal size from below. The base of the dome, inaccessible to marauders, still retains its jewels and one of the most moving moments in the day's changing light comes as the setting sun reaches and lights up the sparkling stones one by one. The floral inlays, possibly the outstanding decorative feature, are world renowned.

Yet when the garden has been exhausted, there is still much to see. The journey on the ferry-boat looks perilous but must surely be one of the most worthwhile in the world. From the opposite bank, the landscape becomes once more one of buildings, river and sky, with

Detail of the reflecting tank.

Early morning.

173

The Taj Mahal from across the river.

the superb effects of light which Agra's humid climate generates. Even the retaining wall to the Jumna is richly decorated on the outside, while the massive garden walls, with their elaborate castellations, are of interest in themselves.

Upon the west, outside the walls, traces remain of many structures, carefully recorded upon Colonel Hodgson's plan. Ruined buildings and arched gates, a cistern, and a raised water course of considerable height, extend down half the garden, while to the south lies yet

another pavilion, the Saheli Burj, one of four pavilions outside the walls.

Many names have figured as designers and craftsmen at the Taj Mahal. Geronimo Veroneo the Venetian goldsmith, the silversmith Austin of Bordeaux, the 'Persians' Ustad Ahmad and Ustad Hamid, have in turn been credited with much of the responsibility. Yet in the last analysis it is most probable that the major influence, the driving intelligence, was that of Shah Jahan himself.

AURANGZIB 1658–1707

With Shah Jahan's illness in 1657, Aurangzib embarked upon a contest of power from which he finally emerged the unchallenged victor. In the course of it he had deposed and imprisoned his father and brought about the deaths of his three brothers, Dara Shukoh, Murad and Shah Suja. Of infinitely stronger character than his rivals, his political skill and military experience were also greater. Yet whatever their respective competence as rulers, in the matter of gardens one cannot but regret the loss of Dara Shukoh. In this respect at least, here might have been another emperor in the pattern of Jahangir and Shah Jahan. Peri Mahal and the garden at Bijbehara are a token of his interest and skill, while the paintings in his Album have delighted succeeding generations.

Differing entirely from his predecessors, Aurangzib personified the type, recurrent through the ages, of the puritan zealot driven by the desire to do good. A controversial figure, his motives must nevertheless be respected. The strict enforcement of the principles of Islam was his aim, and the orthodoxy of Shah Jahan was succeeded by a rigidity amounting at times to oppression. Hindus, Jews and Christians were all to feel, in various ways, the weight of his disapproval, while Muslim deviationists suffered perhaps most of all. Wardens were appointed, in the principal centres of population, charged with the supervision of moral conduct. Drinking, gambling, the taking of opium, dancing and music were all to be discouraged; prayer and fasting were to be faithfully observed. Art and poetry, though not officially disapproved, received little support.

Aurangzib's contribution to architecture was however considerable. It consisted largely of mosques, and of these, the Moti Masjid in the Red Fort at Delhi is of outstanding quality. Of landscape it is probably not unfair to say that he was unaware of its existence as an art and the few gardens laid out in his reign show clearly how the standards of design had begun to degenerate. Yet the Shalamar Bagh at Delhi must have held an attraction for him, for it was here that he was provisionally crowned as emperor, upon the deposition of his father. Later the coronation ceremony was carried out more formally in the Fort at Delhi.

In the context of garden making, his long reign is of interest chiefly for the light it throws on the achievements and customs of his predecessors. The zenith had been reached with Shah Jahan, Aurangzib's own contribution was minimal. Without however the

The three younger sons of Shah Jahan riding together: Shah Suja, Murad and Aurangzib.

The Moti Masjid in the Red Fort at Delhi : the steps to the interior. The pavings throughout are exceptionally fine.

Moti Masjid : the inner courtyard.

178

records of such writers as Bernier, Tavernier and Manucci, much would have been missing from our appreciation of Mughul gardens and of their makers.

François Bernier, a French physician, had reached India on his travels. He first received an offer of service with Dara Shukoh, then already in considerable distress and in flight from his brother. Such however were the straits to which the prince had been reduced that he was unable to provide for Bernier, who instead joined the retinue of Danishmand Khan, one of Aurangzib's nobles. In this capacity Bernier travelled extensively throughout India, and followed in the emperor's train on the occasion of his only visit to Kashmir. Educated and articulate, Bernier has left the most complete descriptions, not only of the Indian cities, but of the gardens of Kashmir itself, and of the fantastic paraphernalia of travel.

Aurangzib had been seriously ill, and decided to visit Kashmir for the sake of his health. Of all the journeys, this was perhaps the most elaborate and the most fully documented. Astrologers were consulted as to the most suitable date to begin the venture and settled upon December 6th, 1664. The visit was to take eighteen months and the first halt was made at the Shalamar Bagh in Delhi, where the travellers remained for six days in order that no preparation for such a momentous journey should be overlooked.

There were many who had doubts about the whole affair:

'. . . the more intelligent sort of men would hardly be persuaded, that as long as he kept his father, Chah-Jean, prisoner in the Fort at Agra, he would think it safe to be at such a distance. Yet not-withstanding we have found, that Reason of State hath given place to that of Health, or rather to the Intrigues of Rauchenara-Begum, who was wild to breath a more free Air than that of the Seraglio, and to have her turn in showing herself to a gallant and magnificent Army, as her sister Begum-Sahed had formerly done during the reign of Chah-Jean.'

The size of the procession was prodigious:

'He hath with him not only the Thirty-five thousand Horse, or thereabout, and 10,000 Foot, but also both his Artilleries, the great or heavy, and the small or lighter, which is called the Artillery of the Stirrup, because it is inseparable from the person of the King, whereas the Heavy sometimes leaveth him to keep the high and well beaten Roads.'

The great artillery required the efforts not merely of twenty yoke of oxen, but of elephants 'when they stick in any deep way, or are to pass some steep mountain'. When one considers two processions of recent times, the Coronation procession of Elizabeth II and the funeral procession of Winston Churchill, and the months of planning required to take them over a few miles of level roads, the logistics of the almost annual migrations to Kashmir are formidable.

They proceeded at leisure, taking nearly two months to travel from Delhi to Lahore. Aurangzib diverted himself with hunting on the way and court business was also carried on periodically as the procession came to rest. Aurangzib followed Akbar's precedent of sending on advance parties, so that all might be in readiness upon his arrival.

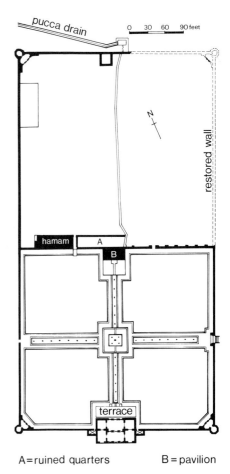

A = ruined quarters   B = pavilion

Plan of the garden at Rajauri on the route to Kashmir.

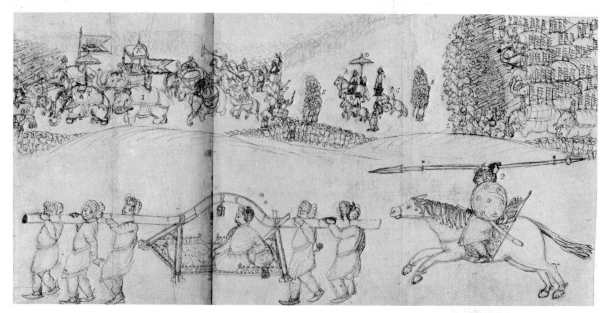

A progress of Shah Jahan in 1632: sketch by Peter Mundy. Shah Jahan, mounted and with an umbrella over his head, is in the middle background. In the left foreground is a palanquin suspended from a thick bamboo which had been artificially made to grow crooked.

Opposite, above: *A sketch by Peter Mundy of the various modes of transporting women in India, starting before birth. The various forms of conveyance shown are Dowlees (doli) – (F); Coaches – (H); Cojavas (kajawa) – (I); Ambarrees (ambari) – (K); Chowndolees (chaundoli) – (L).*

Opposite, below: *Map of routes into Kashmir used by the Mughuls.*

'When the King is in the field, he hath usually two Camps, I mean two Bodies, of Tents separated, to the end that when he breaketh up and leaveth one, the other may have passed before by a day, and be found ready when he arriveth at the place design'd to encamp it: And 'tis therefore, that they are called *Peiche-Kanes*, as if you should say, Houses going before.'

The *peiche-kanes* were virtually identical, each requiring over sixty elephants, two hundred camels, and a hundred mules, together with the necessary porters. They were laid out to an orderly and regular pattern, much as in Akbar's day, and the great lamp, the Akas Diya, was still in use as a beacon.

Apart from the accommodation needed for the retinue itself, and all the various baggage animals,

. . . there must needs be a retreat for all that great number of Birds of prey that are always carried for Game and Magnificence; and so there must be for those many Dogs, and those Leopards serving to take wild Goats; for those Nilgaus, or gray Oxen, . . . for those Lions and Rhinoceros, that are led for greatness; for those great Bufalos of Bengale fighting with Lions; and lastly for those tamed wild Goats, they call Gazelles, that are made to sport before the King.'

Bernier goes on to describe the various methods of transporting the emperor himself, and the royal ladies . . .

'Ordinarily he causeth himself to be carried on mens shoulders, in a kind of Sedan or Litter, upon which is a *Tact-raven*, that is, a Field-throne, on which he is seated: And this is like a magnificent Tabernacle with pillars, painted and guilded, which may be shut with glass, when 'tis ill weather; the four branches of the Litter are cover'd with Scarlet or purpled Gold, with great Gold and Silk-fringes; and at each branch there are two robust and well-cloathed Porters, that change by turns with as many more that follow.'

'Sometimes also he goeth on Horse-back, especially when 'tis a fair day for hunting. At other times he rideth on an Elephant, in a *Mik-dember*, or *Hauze*; and this is the most splendid appearance; For, the Elephant is decked with a very rich and very magnificent Harnass; the *Mik-dember*, being a little square House or Turret of Wood, is alwayes painted and guilded; and the *Hauze*, which is an Oval seat, having a Canopy with Pillars over it, is so likewise.'

'The Princesses, and the great Ladies of the *Seraglio* are also carried in sundry fashions; some are carried, like the King, on mens shoulders, in a *Tchaudoule*, which is a kind of *Tactraven*, painted, guilded, and cover'd with great and costly Net-work of Silk of divers colours, enriched with Embroidery, Fringe, and thick pendant tufts. Others are carried in a very handsome *Palekys* closed, that are likewise painted and guilded, and covered with that rich silken net-work. Some are carried in large Litters by two strong Camels, or by two small Elephants, instead of Mules: and in this manner I have sometimes seen carried *Rauchenara-Begum*; when I also observed, that in the fore-part of her Litter, being open, there was a little She-slave, that with a peacocks-tail kept off from her the Flyes and Dust.'

Upon arriving at the mountains, the numbers in the procession were strictly limited, in order not to make excessive demands upon the provisions available in Kashmir. Even those permitted to accompany the emperor could only take a quarter of their attendants, while the great mass of minor officials, merchants and shopkeepers were left behind. The camels, too, had to be dispensed with, 'these mountains being too steep and craggy for their long shanked and stiff legs'. The elephants however remained essential. Even this greatly reduced party still required some thirty-thousand porters. The route they followed was that used by successive emperors since Akbar, by way of Bhimbar, Rajauri and the Pir Panjal Pass. The original Imperial Road, often carried on embankments or through cuttings, had been progressively improved, and a number of notable *sarais*, or rest houses, had been constructed from the days of Jahangir onwards.

Of these the Changas, Thanna and Aliabad sarais were among the finest. North of Changas, at Rajauri, where Jahangir died, there was even a garden. Built on the traditional Mughul plan, this had a central tank and pavilion, octagonal towers at the four corners, and a bath-house.

The Pir Panjal Pass itself, at 11,400 feet was the lowest point in the mountains south-west of Kashmir. Many travellers have written of its bitter winds, its physical and mental terrors. From this point however began the descent to the Aliabad *sarai*, and thence on down to the inhabited valley. Once arrived at Srinagar, Bernier made a number of excursions, and to these we owe the accounts of Shalamar, Achabal and Vernag which give invaluable clues to their original appearance.

Aurangzib visited Kashmir once only, and the rest of his long reign was spent in India. Each of the emperors has come to be associated with certain cities above all. Babur is remembered at Kabul and Agra; the fugitive Humayun, in his death at least, at Delhi. Agra and Fatehpur Sikri were Akbar's cities, while perhaps Lahore belongs

most to Jahangir, though his real love was always Kashmir. Shah Jahan's Delhi and Agra finally provided the crowning glories of the whole Mughul achievement.

Aurangzib, too, is commemorated by a city. He set up Aurangabad as his southern capital, convenient for his military campaigns. Here he built a citadel, the Kila Arh, and held court attended by over fifty princes, with many thousands of retainers. Two gardens here recall his name. One, the Pan Chakki water-mill, contains the tomb of a Chishti saint who was his spiritual mentor, while north-east of the town lies the tomb-garden of his wife.

The Mausoleum of Rabi A Daurani appears to have been based on the design of the Taj Mahal. The concept is the same, a canal leading up to a domed building, supported by smaller domes and minarets. There however the resemblance ends. The splendour and utter certainty of the Taj Mahal are replaced by a confusion of elements and a weakness of proportion which show clearly that the climax in design had been passed, and that the inevitable decline had set in.

The Mausoleum of Rabi a Daurani, built by Aurangzib at Aurangabad in the Deccan, as a memorial to his first wife.

183

Roshanara Gardens, Delhi: the pavilion is all that survives.

At Lahore, Aurangzib's Badshahi mosque is unusual in having a garden. His daughter, Zebanissa Begam built two gardens here also, the Chau-Burgi Bagh and the Nawan Kot Bagh, but little trace of either remains.

Better remembered, both for her garden and her personality, is Roshanara Begam. Lively and enterprising, this younger daughter of Shah Jahan was rather surprisingly an ardent supporter of her brother Aurangzib. The Roshanara Gardens, once her pleasure garden, must today be searched out in the north-western suburbs of Shahjahanabad. The design, a pavilion and four canals, had already been much altered by 1912, and the original classic pattern blurred with winding drives and flower-beds. She herself comes vividly to life again in Bernier's pages, with her elephants and her escorts, her friendship a passport to success and position in Aurangzib's court. Manucci indeed is not above hinting at scandal:

'I knew that in this journey Rashan Ara Begam did not take in her litter her maid-servant, but in the latter's place a youth dressed as a maid-servant. God knows what they were up to in addition to drinking wine.'

One garden only of the period can compare with the great pleasure gardens of Kashmir or Lahore, Fadai Khan's garden-palace at Pinjaur, near Simla. For this was a reign of religious conflict and constant war, with a ruler disinclined to spare time or resources for the provision of delight.

In 1707, at eighty-nine, the aged emperor died. He had governed for nearly fifty years, with courage and authority to the last. His ceaseless military campaigns left the empire larger territorially at his death than at his accession, but the tensions engendered by his policies were to prove a major contribution to its decline and disappearance. With Aurangzib, the dynamic of the Mughuls approached its end. The empire ceased to be effective in the 1750s, but outwardly, in ever-diminishing form, it survived to reach its final figure-head in Bahadur Shah II (r. 1837–57) maintaining his little court at Delhi in the shadow of the British presence in India.

PINJAUR, NEAR SIMLA

Fadai Khan, Aurangzib's foster-brother, had directed the construction of the Imperial Mosque at Lahore, and appears to have been one of the few men for whom the emperor had any real warmth of regard. When he received the governorship of Pinjaur, in the Himalayan foothills, he resolved to build himself a splendid garden in the tradition of Jahangir.

Udaipur: the Sahelion-ki-Dari, or Garden of the Maids of Honour, who by tradition were sent by the emperor to the Maharana, reversing the more usual process. The date is uncertain, but it is probably rather late. On top of the small pavilion on the right – one of a pair – a small metal bird revolves while the fountains play.

Pinjaur. The original symmetry of the building has been distorted by subsequent additions.

Legend records a very ancient garden on this site, and the first historical record goes back to AD 1030. A garden here is reputed to have been destroyed by Timur, and the site remained a wilderness until Fadai Khan laid out the present garden. This again became derelict, and was restored by the rulers of Patiala during the last century. The modern city of Chandigarh lies thirteen miles away.

The site is magnificent, looking across a fertile valley ringed by hills. Unlike most Mughul gardens, the entrance is from the higher ground, and the seven terraces step down the hill, revealing a fresh view at each level. The steepness of the site allows impressive falls between each terrace, and the central water-course is strong and dominant, but it lacks the subtlety of earlier gardens. It also lacks their sense of intimacy. The mango orchards on each side of the lower terraces are not high enough to give enclosure, and the un-planted lower part of the garden is rather bleak and open.

The calm symmetry of the Mughul pavilions has also suffered from extensions built in the last century. Nevertheless in scale and concept it is a *tour-de-force* and when the water is flowing (which it does on occasions) the effect must be magnificent. At other times it suffers more from the lack of water than many of the earlier gardens, where perfection of design can bear even that loss.

Opposite: *The cascade at Pinjaur. At night, lighted candles in the recesses, or* chini-kanas, *glittered through the solid sheet of water.*

187

PLANT MATERIAL IN THE MUGHUL GARDENS

From the Mughuls themselves, we know that their gardens were full of flowers, fruit and trees. Contemporary sources are their memoirs, their paintings, and plants and flowers of every kind in the inlays, carvings and mural paintings of their buildings. The memoirs of Babur and Jahangir are filled with details of their gardens. While much research is still needed to identify with certainty many of the plants to which they refer, it is possible to build up a fairly general picture of the materials they used.

In the paintings trees and flowers abound, the chenar and the cypress especially, spring flowers scatter the gardens, and branches of fruit blossom overhang the walls. The portraits of the emperors show them with flowers at their feet, while the margins of both paintings and manuscripts are decorated with exquisite botanical detail. Carvings in bas-relief give expression to the form and growth of the plants which are their subjects, while the pietra-dura inlays, such as those at the Taj Mahal, add colour to complete their astonishingly lifelike illustrations.

Some information too is available from European travellers in the Mughul Empire. They, however, were primarily interested in the life and buildings around them, and when they write of plants, it is usually in general terms. They may refer, for instance, to roses or lilies, but give little indication of species or variety.

Bernier records his impressions as he left the plains in the train of Aurangzib, crossed the mountains, and began the descent into Kashmir:

Opposite: *A crown imperial from Dara Shukoh's album.*

Below: *The flower paintings in this border of a miniature show considerable realism, yet elude identification.*

The champa – Michelia champaca, *mentioned by both Jahangir and Abu-'l-Fazl. From the Roxburgh collection at the Royal Botanic Gardens, Kew.*

The kesu – Butea frondosa. *Also called* dhak *or* palas.

'It seem'd to me surprising enough, to find myself from the first night that we parted from Bember, and entred into the Mountains, pass from a Torrid to a Temperate Zone. For, we had no sooner mounted this dreadful Wall of the World, I mean, this high, steep, black and bald Mountain, of Bember, but that in descending on the other side, we found an Air that was pretty tollerable, fresh, gentle and temperate. But that which surprised me more in these Mountains, was, to find myself, in a trice, transported out of the Indies into Europe. For, seeing the Earth covered with all our plants and shrubs, except Issop, Thyme, Marjoram and Rosemary, I imagined I was in some of our Mountains of Auvergne, in the midst of a Forest of all our kinds of Trees, Pines, Oaks, Elms, Plane-trees. And I was the more astonish'd because in all those burning Fields of Indostan, whence I came, I had seen almost nothing of all that.'

Yet it is surprising, in view of the difference in climate, how many species are found in both the Indian plains and in Kashmir. The emperors were active particularly in the import of fruit trees, while the tradition of planting shade trees is centuries old. As successive rulers built roads, so they planted avenues along them. At halting places, the trees were often extended four-square, so as to provide shade from all points of the compass. Wherever possible, a well would also be constructed at these halts.

Sebastien Manrique's description of the approach to Sehrind, a royal garden in Patiala state, gives a pleasant picture of coolness contrived out of heat:

'I took the opportunity to visit the Royal gardens at this place, belonging to the Mogol Emperor. . . . One passes to it along a most lovely road, or rather avenue, some forty feet wide, and ornamented on both sides with fresh green willows planted at regular intervals. Their branches met above and, interlacing, form a green leafy canopy. . . . Along one side of this pleasant avenue flows a rivulet. . . . The avenue ends in a wide open plain where the garden is situated. It was square in form, divided into equal sections each covering about half a league, the whole enclosed by a high massive wall of strong burnt bricks. Four lofty sumptuous gateways lead into this most pleasant fruit garden. Each gateway, when open, gives a vista down a long wide roadway, the four forming a cross; one could not see from one end to the other. These roads are ornamented at regular intervals by funereal obelisk-shaped cypresses which divide the garden into four sections: one section contains every kind of fruit tree; a second every kind of flower and odoriferous herb in abundance; in the third section are eatable vegetables of all kinds, and in the last section a grand Royal Palace. . . .'

Widely used in Kashmir were such shade trees as oriental plane, cypress, willow and poplar; while in the plains would be added palms, mango, tamarind, and the ubiquitous *champa* or pagoda tree. The mango, described by Babur as 'the best fruit in Hindustan', served the dual purpose of providing both deep shade and delicious fruit.

Peter Mundy tells us that when Jahangir planted the road-side avenues stretching out from Agra, he used Nim (*Margosa*), pipal (*Ficus religiosa*), dhak (*Butea frondosa*) and bahr (*Ficus indica*) 'for the ease of Travellers, and for shade in hott weather'.

The planting of fruit trees was held in great regard, both for its own sake and for the revenue it produced. Much detail is available on the introduction of fruit from one country to another, and of its subsequent culture. Akbar, for instance, arranged for the import of apple trees from Samarkand, even though in Agra they needed to be watered nine months of the year. Even Humayun took the trouble to visit his distant orange gardens.

In present-day Kashmir, the abundance of fruit of all kinds, and particularly the excellence of the walnuts, tallies very closely with the descriptions of the Mughuls.

Jahangir writes of Kashmir:

'Before my father's time there were no *shah-alu* (cherries). Muhammad Zuli Afshar brought them from Kabul and planted them, and there are now ten or fifteen fruit-bearing trees. There were also some apricot trees. The aforesaid made them known in this country, and now there are many of them. In fact the apricot of Kashmir is good. . . . There are pears (*nashpat*) of the best kind, better than Kabul, or Badakhshan and nearly equal to those of Samarkand. The apples of Kashmir are celebrated for their goodness. The guavas (*amrud*) are middling. Grapes are plentiful but most of them are harsh and inferior, and the pomegranates are not worth much. Water-melons of the best kind can be obtained. . . . There are no *shah-tut* (some kind of large mulberry) but there are other (*tut*) mulberries everywhere. From the foot of every mulberry-tree a vine-creeper grows up.'

One is reminded of the plain of Lombardy, where the mulberry trees supporting one great industry, of silk, were looped with vines, the symbol of another.

Even a short list of fruit from Mughul records would produce:

The chaltah – Dillenia speciosa.

Almond	Guava	Pineapple
Apple	Lemon	Plantain
Apricot	Lime	(banana)
Cherry	Mango	Plum
(sweet and sour)	Melon	Pomegranate
Citron	Mulberry	Quince
Coconut	Orange	Sugar-cane
Date	(sweet and sour)	Walnut
Fig	Peach	Watermelon
Grape	Pear	

Babur, writing in 1526, described in great detail the merits and demerits of various Indian fruits: the *mahuwa*, from which araq was distilled, jack-fruit, corinda, and many others. Of date liquor he remarked: 'No hilarity was felt, much must be drunk, seemingly, to produce a little cheer.'

In the choice of flowers, colour and scent were all-important, although symbolism also played some part.

'From the excellencies of its sweet-scented flowers one may prefer the fragrances of India to those of the flowers of the whole world. It has many such that nothing in the whole world can be compared to them. The first is the *champa* [*Michelia champaca*], which is a flower of exceedingly sweet fragrance; it has the shape of the

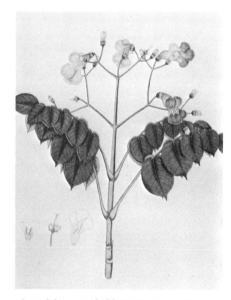

The padal *was probably* Stereospermum suavolens.

191

Above, left: *An illustrated copy of the* Babur-nama *in the British Museum contains accurate portrayals of birds, animals and plants, such as the screwpine at the bottom of this page;* right, *a* Mimusops *from the same* Babur-nama. *Shapely evergreen trees of this size seem to have been among the Mughul's favourites.*

saffron flower, but is yellow inclining to white. The tree is very symmetrical and large, full of branches and leaves and is shady. When in flower one tree would perfume a garden. Surpassing this is the *keora* flower [*Pandanus odoratissimus*]. Its shape and appearance are singular, and its scent so strong and penetrating that it does not yield to the odour of musk. Another is the *rae bel* [may be a jessamine] which in scent resembles white jessamine. Its flowers are double and treble. Another is the *mulsari* [*Mimusops Elengi*]. This tree too is very graceful and symmetrical and is shady. The scent of its flowers is very pleasant. Another is the *ketaki* [?*Pandanus*] which is of the nature of the *keora*, but the latter is thorny, whereas the *ketki* has no thorns. . . . Moreover the *ketki* is yellowish, whereas the *keora* is white. From these two flowers and also from the *chambeli* [*Jasminum grandiflorum*] which is the white jessamine of *wilayat* [Persia or Afghanistan], they extract sweet-scented oils. There are other flowers too numerous to mention. Of trees there are the cypress [*sarw*], the pine [*sambar*] the *chanar* [*Platanus orientalis*], the white poplar [*safidar, Populus alba*] and the *bid mulla* [willow], which they had never formerly thought of in Hindustan, but are now plentiful. The sandal-tree, which once was peculiar to the islands [i.e. Java, Sumatra, etc] also flourishes in the gardens. . . .'

Jahangir

Yet revenue too was not without significance. The saffron crop of Kashmir has for centuries been important economically; while the gardens of Lake Dal in Jahangir's day produced a substantial income from roses and bed musk.

A long tradition of flower festivals exists in Kashmir, with the lilac, the rose and the lotus each in turn attracting its admirers. Few flowers can have a more ancient symbolism than the lotus, the sacred flower of both Hindu and Buddhist. From Egypt to the Far East, it has been held in reverence for centuries. It is the symbol of creation; and of the various species found in India the rose-coloured lotus of Lake Dal is especially the symbol of sunrise.

It was upon the lotus lily bud, rising from the surface of the water, that the Mughuls based the design of fountain jets. Their fountains were composed from patterns of water, rather than from the sculptures, rocks and vases of their European contemporaries, so that the jet itself was all-important, and the lotus bud became an almost invariable component of their designs.

The flowers used in the miniatures and inlays are often so stylized as to be unrecognizable. Some of them were probably copied from Persian manuscripts, but there are many that are true portraits. Among these are cyclamen, iris, tulips, crown imperials, lilies, pinks, roses, poppies and peonies. From European records we might add:

Region of Delhi and Agra	*Kashmir and Lahore*
Carnation	Carnation
Coxcomb	Delphinium
Heliotrope	Hollyhock
Hyacinth	Jasmine
Jasmine	Lilac
Larkspur	Lotus
Love-lies-bleeding	Narcissus
Lotus	Saffron
Marigolds	Stocks
Narcissus	Wallflower
Oleanders	
Tuberoses	
Violet	
Zinnia	

Many plants are named in the memoirs of Babur and Jahangir and in the *Ain-i-Akbari*. Lists taken from these sources are given below with such identification as is at present available; reasonably firm identifications are given in small capitals.

Rewarding work awaits some scholar who would delve more deeply into these sources and in so doing would perhaps enable more of the original species to be restored to the gardens.

The dhanantar – Clitoria ternates.

Hibiscus cannabinus.

LIST OF PLANT NAMES

I From the Memoirs of Babur

AMLA
: MYROBALAN TREE – PHYLLANTHUS EMBLICA *(Euphorbiacae)* – deciduous small to medium tree, grown for its fruit

ANBAH
: MANGO

ANBLI
: TAMARIND – TAMARINDUS INDICA *(Leguminosae)* – date tree

BADHAL
: MONKEY-JACK – ARTOCARPUS LACOOCHA – medium deciduous tree

BER
: LOTE FRUIT – ZIZYPHUS JUJUBA *(Rhamnaceae)*

CHIKDA
: RED JUJUBE – ELEAGNUS ANGUSTIFOLIA *(Eleagnaceae)*

CHIRUNJI
: BUCHANANIA LATIFOLIA *(Anacardinaceae)* – medium deciduous tree

GULAR
: CLUSTERED FIG – FICUS GLOMERATA *(Moraceae)*

JAMAN
: EUGENIA JAMBOLANA *(Myrtaceae)* – medium evergreen tree

JASUN
: HIBISCUS ROSA SINENSIS *(Malvaceae)*

KADHIL
: JACK-FRUIT – ARTOCARPUS INTEGRIFOLIA *(Moraceae)* – large evergreen tree

KAMRAK
: AVERRHON CARAMBOELA *(Geraniaceae)* – a tree cultivated for its fruit

KANIR
: OLEANDER – NERIUM ODORUM *(Apocynaceae)*

KARAUNDA
: CORINDA – CARISSA CARANDAS *(Apocynaceae)* – large evergreen shrub

KARDI
: a special kind of peach

KELA
: PLANTAIN – MUSA PARADAISICA SAPIENTUM *(Scitamineae)*

KHIRNI
: MIMUSOPS KAUKI *(Sapotaceae)* – evergreen tree of medium height

KHURMA
: DATE PALM – PHOENIX DACTYLIFERA *(Palmae)*

KIURA
: SCREWPINE – PANDANUS ODORATISSIMUS *(Pandanaceae)* – shrub or small tree, up to 20 ft, with aerial roots

LIMU
: LIME – CITRUS ACIDA *(Rutaceae)*

MAHUWA
: BASSIA LATIFOLIA *(Sapotaceae)* – a deciduous tree 40–50 ft high. Arak was distilled from the flowers. Also called *gul-chikan*

NARANJ
: ORANGE – CITRUS AURANTIUM *(Rutaceae)*

NARGIL
: COCONUT PALM – COCOS NUCIFERA *(Palmae)*

PANIYALA
: FLACOURTIA CATAPHRACTA *(Flacourtiaceae)* – medium deciduous tree, possibly red-apple

QAWUN
: MUSK-MELON

SANGTARA
: and other forms of citrus trees

TAR
: PALMYRA PALM – BORASSUS FLABELLIFORMIS *(Palmae)*

TURUNJ
: CITRON – CITRUS MEDICA *(Rutaceae)*

YASMAN
: JASMINE

II From the Memoirs of Jahangir

BID MULLA
: WILLOW

CHAMBELI
: JASMINE – JASMINUM GRANDIFLORUM

CHAMPA
: PAGODA TREE – MICHELIA CHAMPACA *(Magnoliaceae)* – large evergreen tree

CHENAR
: ORIENTAL PLANE – PLATANUS ORIENTALIS *(Platanaceae)*

KEORA
: SCREWPINE – PANDANUS ODORATISSUMUS

KETKI or KETAKI
: *Keora* (see above)

MULSARI
: MIMUSOPS ELENGI *(Sapotaceae)* – evergreen tree of medium height

RAE BEL
: JASMINE – JASMINUM ZAMBAC *(Oleinaceae)*

SAFIDAR
: WHITE POPLAR – POPULUS ALBA *(Salicaceae)*

SARW
: CYPRESS – CUPRESSUS SEMPERVIRENS *(Coniferae)*

III From the Ain-i-Akbari, by Abu-'l-Fazl

A list of fine smelling flowers:

BHOLSARI
: *Mimusops elengi* (This seems to be a corruption of *mulsari*)

CHALTAH
: DILLENIA SPECIOSA OR INDICA *(Dilleniaceae)* – flowering tree

CHAMBELI	JASMINUM GRANDIFLORUM
CHAMPA	MICHELIA CHAMPACA
GULAL	Gulal is the red powder used at Holi. *Gulal tulsi* is *Ocimum Basilicum* (*Labiateae*), sweet basil; *Gulali* is *Crotalaria medicaginea* (*Leguminosae*)
GUL I ZA'FARAN	SAFFRON – CROCUS SATIVUS
JUHI	JASMINUM AURICULATUM
KAPUR BEL	*Japanese camphor tree – Cinnamonum camphora* (*Laurinaceae*) – evergreen
KARNAH	A species of citron, very fragrant
KETKI	PANDANUS ODORATISSIMUS
KEWARAH	Probably a corruption of *keora* (see above)
KUZAH	Possibly a rose of some sort – used for making perfumes
MONGRA	Munga? – *Moringa pterygosperma* or *Hyperanthera moringa* (*Moringaceae*)
NARGIS	NARCISSUS
NIWARI	*Jasminum zambac* or *Jasminum elongatum*
PADAL	*Stereospermum suavolens* (*Bignonaceae*) – medium deciduous tree
RAIBEL	JASMINUM ZAMBAC
SEWTI	ROSA GLANDULIFERA
SINGHARAR	The Persian text clearly has SINGARHAR – NYCTANTHES ARBOR TRISTIS (*Oleaceae*) – large deciduous shrub or small tree grown for the fragrant evening scent of its flowers
TASBIH I GULAL	
VIOLET	*Violet*

A list of flowers notable for their beauty:

BHUN CHAMPA	*Michelia kisopa* or *Koemferia rotunda* (*Scitaminae*)
CHAMPALAH	*Quisqualis indica* (*Combretaceae*)? – or possibly an error for *champa* or *chambell*
DHANANTAR	*Clitoria ternatea* (*Leguminosae*)
DUPAHRIYA	*Dupari?* – *Pentapetes phoenicea* (*Sterculiaceae*)
GUDHAL	Probably *gurhal* – shoe flower – *Hibiscus syriacus* (*Malvaceae*) – a shrubby mallow also known as *Althea frutex*

GUL I A'FTAB	SUNFLOWER – HELIANTHUS ANNUUS
GUL I HINNA	*Lawsonia inermis* (*Lythraceae*)
GUL I KANWAL	LOTUS – NYMPHAEA NELUMBO or NYMPHAEA ALBA (*Nymphaceae*)
GUL I KARAUNDAH	*Corinda* (see KARAUNDA above)
GUL I MALTI	*Jasminum officinalis*
JA'FARI	*Linum trigynum* (*Linaceae*) according to Platts, but *Tagetes patula* (marigold) (*Compositae*) according to A. Constable
JAIT	*Sesbania aegyptica* (*Leguminosae*) – a small deciduous tree, or *Aeschynomene sesban* (*Leguminosae*) – a water plant
KADAM	*Nauclea cadamba* (*Rubiaceae*) or *Mitragyna parvifolia* (*Rubiaceae*)
KANER	OLEANDER – *Nerium odorum* or *indicum*
KANGLAI	*Kanglu?* – *Sponia politoria* (*Urticaceae*) or *Kangli* – *Sida populifolia* or *indica* (*Malvaceae*)
KARIL	Caper – CAPPARIS APHYLLA (*Capparideae*)
KARN P'HUL	*Karanphal?* – Citron. The fragrant fruit was used for scenting apartments
KESU	BUTEA MONOSPERMA or FRONDOSA (*Leguminosae*) – *dhak* or *palas* – small or medium tree
LAHI	*lai?* – *Tamarix* (*Tamaricaceae*)
NAGESKAR	*Nagkesar* – MESUA FERREA (*Guttiferae*)
RATANMALA	The juice was used as a dye
RATANMANJANI	Probably a climbing plant
SAN	*Hibiscus cannabinus* (*Malvaceae*) or *Cannabis sativa* (*Urticaceae*)
SENBAL	*Semal* – silk cotton tree – *Bombax heptaphyllum* (*Malvaceae*) – deciduous
SIRI K'HANDI	A climbing plant, possibly a small form of jasmine
SIRS	*Albizzia lebbek* or *odoratissima* (*Leguminaceae*) or *Acacia sirisa* (*Leguminosae*)
SONZARD	A climbing plant?
SUDARSAN	ROSE APPLE – EUGENIA JAMBU
SURPAN	ALEXANDRIAN LAUREL – CALLOPHYLLUM INOPHYLLUM (*Guttiferae*)

BIBLIOGRAPHY

ABU-'L-FAZL IBN MUBARAK, called ALLAMI, *Ain-i-Akbari*, Vol. I translated by H. Blochmann, Vols. II and III by H. S. Jarrett, Asiatic Society of Bengal, Calcutta, 1873–94.

ABU-'L-FAZL IBN MUBARAK, The *Akbar-nama*, Vol. III, translated by Henry Beveridge, Asiatic Society of Bengal, Calcutta, 1939.

ARBERRY, A. J., ed., *The legacy of Persia*, Oxford University Press, London, 1953.

BABUR, *The Babur-nama in English* (Memoirs of Babur), translated by A. P. Beveridge, Luzac & Co., London, 1922.

BADAONI, *Mutakhabu Tawarikh*, Vol. II, translated by W. H. LOWE, Asiatic Society of Bengal, Calcutta, 1884.

BAMBER, C. J., *Plants of the Punjab*, Punjab Government Press, 1916.

BAQIR, M., *Lahore past and present*, Panjab University Press, 1952.

BERNIER, FRANCOIS, *Collection of Travels through Turky into Persia and the East Indies . . . being the travels of Monsieur Tavernier Bernier and other great men*. Published for Moses Pitt at the Angel in St Paul's Churchyard, London, 1684.

BRANDIS, D., *Indian trees*, Constable, London, 1906.

DE CLAVIJO, R. G., *Narrative of the Embassy of Ruy Gonzales de Clavijo to the Court of Timour at Samarcand, AD 1403–6*, translated by C. R. Markham, Hakluyt Society, series I, no. 26, London, 1870.

ELLIOT AND DOWSON, *The history of India as told by its own historians*, London, 1867–77.

Encyclopaedia Britannica, Jammu and Kashmir.

FERGUSON, J. P., *Kashmir*, Centaur Press, London, 1961.

FERGUSSON, J., *History of Indian and Eastern Architecture*, John Murray, London, 1876.

FOSTER, W., ed., *Early travels in India*, Oxford University Press, London, 1921.

FOSTER, W., ed., *The embassy of Sir Thomas Roe to India*, Oxford University Press, London, 1926.

GOETZ, H., *Five thousand years of Indian Art* (Art of the World No. 1), Methuen, London, 1959.

GULBADAN BEGAM, *The History of Humayun*, or *Humayun-nama*, translated by A. P. Beveridge, Royal Asiatic Society, London, 1902.

HAIDAR, MIRZA MUHAMMAD, DOUGHLAT, *Tarikh-i-Rashidi*, translated by E. Denison Ross, Sampson Lowe, London, 1895.

HUEGEL, BARON C., *Travels in Kashmir and the Panjab*, with notes by T. B. Jervis, London, 1845.

JAHANGIR, *Tuzuk-i-Jahangiri* or *Memoirs of Jahangir*, translated by A. Rogers, edited by H. Beveridge, Royal Asiatic Society, London 1909 and 1914.

JAIRAZBHOY, R. A., Early garden-palaces of the Great Mughals, *Oriental Art*, IV, Summer 1958, pp. 68–75.

KAK, RAM CHANDRA, *Ancient Monuments of Kashmir*, The Indian Society, London, 1933.

KAYE, G. R., *A guide to the old Indian observatories*, Calcutta, 1920.

LATIF, S. M., *Lahore: its history, architectural remains and antiquities*, 1892.

MANRIQUE, S., *The travels of Sebastien Manrique, 1629–43*, Vol. II, Hakluyt Society papers, series II, Vol. LXI, London.

MANUCCI, N., *Storia do Mogor*, translated by W. Irvine, John Murray, London, 1907.

MATHUR, N., *Red Fort and Mughal Life*, National Museum, Delhi, 1964.

MOORCROFT, W., *Travels in the Himalayan provinces of Hindustan and the Panjab; in Ladakh and Kashmir; in Peshawar, Kabul, Munduz and Bokhara, 1819–1825*, ed., G. Trebeck, John Murray, London, 1841.

MUNDY, PETER, *The travels of Peter Mundy in Europe and Asia, 1608–67*, Vol. II, Hakluyt Society Papers, series II, Vol. XXXV, London.

PLATTS, J., *A dictionary of Urdu, classical Hindi and English*, Oxford University Press, London, 5th imp. 1930.

POWELL-PRICE, J. C., *A history of India*, Thomas Nelson, London, 1955.

PRAWDIN, M., *The builders of the Mogul Empire*, Allen & Unwin, London, 1963.

SMITH, E. W., *The tomb of Akbar*, Government Press, United Provinces, 1909.

SPEAR, P., *A history of India*, Vol. II, Penguin Books, Harmondsworth, 1965.

STEIN, M. A., *Notes on the ancient topography of the Pir Pantsal route*, Baptist Mission Press, Calcutta, 1896.

STEIN, M. A., *Memoir on the ancient geography of Kashmir*, Baptist Mission Press, Calcutta, 1899.

STEIN, M. A., *Kalhana's Rajatarangini*, Constable, London, 1900.

TAVERNIER, J. B., *The six travels of John Baptista Tavernier, Baron of Aubonne, through Turkey and Persia to the Indies . . .* made English by J. P., London, 1684.

VIGNE, G. T., *A personal narrative of a visit to Ghuzin, Kabul and Afghanistan*, London, 1840.

VIGNE, G. T., *Travels in Kashmir, Ladak, Iskardo, etc.* Henry Colburn, London, 1842.

VILLIERS-STUART, C. M., *Gardens of the Great Mughals*, A. & C. Black, London, 1913.

WALI ULLA KHAN, M., *Lahore and its important monuments*, Ministry of Education, Government of Pakistan, 1964.

WILBER, D. N., *Persian gardens and garden pavilions*, Charles Tuttle, Rutland, Vermont and Tokyo, Japan, 1962.

ACKNOWLEDGMENTS

PHOTOGRAPHS
All photographs not otherwise attributed are by Susan Jellicoe.

Roderick Cameron, p. 117; Sylvia Crowe, pp. 17, 20; Christina Gascoigne, pp. 34 top, 43, 122 top, 123 bottom, 129 bottom, 143 bottom, 186, 187; M. G. Griffin, p. 31; Sheila Haywood, pp. 30, 34 bottom, 51 bottom, 88, 89, 120 top, 125 bottom, 141 top, 143 top, 163 bottom; India Office Library, pp. 72 top, 136, 158 top, 159, 161 bottom, 169 bottom; Indian Government Tourist Office, London, pp. 23, 25, 36, 53, 78, 83 top, 125 top, 129 top, 162; Michael Lancaster, pp. 72 left, 155 top; Mrs Nemon-Stuart, pp. 71, 86, 98, 99 top, 101 top, 116, 174–5, 183; Gordon Patterson, p. 35; Robert Skelton, pp. 26, 27, 150, 151 top; C. R. V. Tandy, pp. 126, 127, 130, 131 top, 148, 152, 172 top.

MINIATURES, PAINTINGS, ETC.
British Museum, pp. 33, 69, 79, 140, 192; Chester Beatty Collection, Dublin, pp. 41, 67, 91, 124 bottom; India Office Library, pp. 12–13, 37 top, 39, 57, 80, 137 top, 144, 156 top, 189; Capt. Knight (from *Diary of a pedestrian in Cashmere and Thibet*) p. 112; Royal Botanic Gardens, Kew, pp. 190, 191, 193; Royal Institute of British Architects, pp. 124 top, 128; Victoria & Albert Museum (Crown copyright), pp. 15, 24, 52, 58–59, 75, 77, 109, 113, 133, 137 right, 142, 177, 188; G. T. Vigne, pp. 62 (from *A personal narrative of a visit to Ghuzin, Kabul & Afghanistan*), 146 (from *Travels in Kashmir*); C. Villiers-Stuart, p. 97.

PLANS, MAPS, ETC.
All plans and maps not otherwise attributed are by Gordon Patterson, whose measured drawings of the gardens set out their general character but do not purport to be detailed surveys. H. Blochmann, p. 76, 80 (from his translation of vol. I of the *Ain-i-Akbari*); Mary de Chazal, pp. 63 (from plans by R. A. Jairazbhoy), 81 (based on a drawing by H. Blochmann – see above); Sheila Haywood, p. 50; India Office Library, pp. 147, 156 bottom, 168, 179 (from *Antiquities of Bhimbar and Rajauri* by Ram Chandra Kak); Gordon Patterson, pp. 18–19, 22 (drawings based on plans in *Persian gardens and pavilions* by Donald Wilber), p. 85 top (based on a plan in *The tomb of Akbar* by E. W. Smith); Susan Smith, pp. 73 (from a plan in *Delhi – Humayun's tomb and adjacent buildings* by S. A. A. Naqvi); p. 165; C. Villiers Stuart, p. 149 (from *Gardens of the Great Mughals*).

INDEX

Page numbers are in roman type, references to plates in *italic*.
Main references are in **bold** type.